THE CRYSTAL PALACE

THE CRYSTAL PALACE

PETER BERLYN,
CHARLES FOWLER, JR.

ISBN: 978-93-89614-26-8

Published: 1851

LECTOR HOUSE LLP
E-MAIL: lectorpublishing@gmail.com

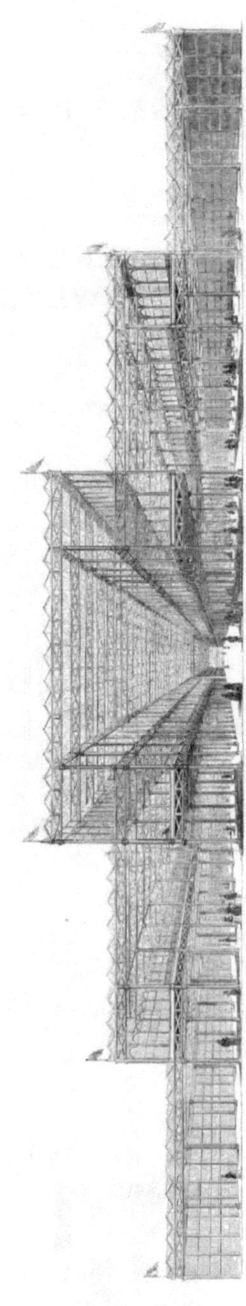

TRANSVERSE SECTION OF THE BUILDING, SHOWING THE INTERIOR COMPLETED.

THE CRYSTAL PALACE.

ITS ARCHITECTURAL HISTORY AND CONSTRUCTIVE MARVELS.

BY

PETER BERLYN,
AND
CHARLES FOWLER, JUNR.

MDCCCLI.

CONTENTS

CONTENTS

LIST OF ILLUSTRATIONS

INTRODUCTORY REMARKS

O much has already been said and written, both wisely and well, upon the marvellous edifice which has just been reared with such magical rapidity to enshrine the results of the skill and industry of all nations, that it would appear an almost hopeless task to present the subject in any new point of view to the reader.

If, therefore, the authors cannot lay claim to novelty or originality in the execution of the pleasurable work which they have undertaken, they are not without hopes that, from their having been connected with this gigantic undertaking during the greater part of its progress, they will be enabled to trace in a more detailed and consecutive manner than has yet been attempted the history of the design and execution of the building up to the period of its completion.

A great deal has been lately said upon the want of distinctive character in almost all the buildings of the present day; and it is certainly a striking fact that in scarcely any of our important modern structures does the exterior appearance in any way lead the spectator to form an idea of the purposes or arrangement of the interior, the former being apparently governed by fancy, or the fashion for some particular style, while the latter only, is accommodated to the peculiar requirements of the case. Thus we have porticos which do not shelter from the weather, or in which no one is allowed to walk; Venetian palaces appear piled upon a substructure of plate-glass; baronial castles prove to be model prisons; and richly-decorated mansions, from the time of "Good Queen Bess," or fanciful Italian villas, are made to serve for the accommodation of paupers.

The ancients appear to have been more careful in this respect, so that the form and external arrangement afforded in most cases a ready key to the purposes of their structures. Their temples, their fora, theatres and amphitheatres, baths, and other public edifices, seem each to have been stamped with their own characteristic features, at the same time without in any way producing a monotonous uniformity among the different examples of the same class of building.

Now, if this criterion of excellence be applied to the remarkable building recently erected in Hyde Park, it will be found that the constructive arrangement of the interior is plainly expressed without, and it must be conceded that it possesses at least those elements of beauty arising from consistency and simplicity which, in combination with its vast size, give it also that of grandeur. That it is faultless it would be needless to assert, or to imagine that, from its example, a new style of architecture will originate; but that it is admirably suited to its purpose, that it is a remarkable specimen of the constructive skill of this country, and that it will certainly form one of the most interesting objects of the Great Exhibition by which it has been called into being, if not the most interesting of all, must, we think, be admitted by all candid observers.

Although the building in its present form was designed, as well as carried out, in a singularly short space of time, this could not have been accomplished but for the great amount of thought and labour which had been previously bestowed upon the subject. In order, therefore, to trace the whole of the progress of the design, it will be necessary briefly to advert to the early labours bestowed upon the project.

On the 5th of January, 1850, the Royal Commission for carrying out this great scheme was gazetted; its first and second meetings, which were respectively held on the 11th and 18th of the same month, were entirely devoted to preliminary arrangements, and determining the mode of conducting its proceedings.

Among the most urgent matters calling for the attention of the Commissioners, the subject of the building early presented itself, as it was of the utmost importance that the longest possible time should be allowed for its erection; and, accordingly, at the third meeting, held on the 24th of January, the following noblemen and gentlemen were appointed to act as a

Committee For All Matters Relating To The Building

His Grace the Duke of BUCCLEUCH, K.G., F.R.S.

The Right Hon. the Earl of ELLESMERE, F.S.A.

CHARLES BARRY, Esq., R.A., F.R.S.

WILLIAM CUBITT, Esq., F.R.S., Pr. of J.C.E.

ROBERT STEPHENSON, Esq., M.P., F.R.S.

C. R. COCKERELL, Esq., R.A.

I. K. BRUNEL, Esq., F.R.S.

THOMAS L. DONALDSON, Esq., M.I.B.A.

From which list it will be seen that some of the very highest professional talent in the country was enlisted on behalf of the undertaking.

LABOURS OF THE BUILDING COMMITTEE

HE first point to be ascertained by this Committee was where to find an eligible site; for although they were not able at that early stage of their labours to determine the exact amount of space that would be required, they appear to have been of opinion that, from the general data before them, about sixteen acres would be necessary—an amount which has been subsequently considerably exceeded, but which was already an enormous area to be covered by one building; and in dealing with it the Committee must have felt that a very heavy amount of responsibility rested upon them, as appears, indeed, from their recommendation to the Royal Commission given below.

After about a month of attentive deliberation, the Committee made a report upon this part of their labours.

With regard to the site, it had appeared to the Committee that—firstly, the north-eastern portion of Hyde Park; secondly, the long space between her Majesty's private road and the Kensington road, in the southern part of Hyde Park; and thirdly, the north-western portion of Regent's Park, were the only available spaces about the metropolis which would afford the necessary accommodation; and it was believed that the order in which they were named represented also their relative eligibility. As regarded the first, the Committee had been informed by the Chief Commissioner of her Majesty's Woods and Forests that considerable objections would arise to its occupation for such a purpose, and that no such objections would be raised to the use of the second; and the Committee, therefore, recommended the adoption of this site, which, amongst other advantages, is remarkable for the facility of access afforded by the existing roads.

As regarded the extent of the building, the Committee were not yet in possession of sufficient data to enable them to determine this accurately, but, from such information as they had before them, they thought that it might be assumed, for the present, that about sixteen acres of covered space would be required.

And finally, as regarded the mode of proceeding to determine the general interior arrangements or ground-plan of the building, a subject to which they had given much consideration, they resolved, "That, in their opinion, it was desirable to seek, by public competition, for suggestions as to the general arrangements of the ground-plan of the building."

It was deemed by the Committee that the peculiar object for which the building was required, namely, the encouragement of the widest and most liberal competition in all the branches of arts and manufactures—the circumstance of the cost of the erection being defrayed by the public—the peculiar character of the building, for the designing of which were especially required judgment and contrivance in the detail of arrangement, and experience in the management of large crowds, and for the construction of which the mechanical skill and knowledge of the application and of the economical use of materials now so generally possessed by builders and practical men were necessary—all seemed, in the opinion of the Committee, to be reasons for recommending that the designs for the general arrangements should, as far as practicable, be the result of public competition, and that the actual construction should be so to the fullest extent. The Committee were, moreover, of opinion that the general design or arrangement of such a building was one of those subjects, perhaps few in number, on which many good ideas may be elicited by a general contribution of plans; and that a mode might be adopted of obtaining such plans, and collecting useful suggestions from them, which should not eventually lead to any loss of time, or be attended with those delays which too frequently render ordinary competition inconvenient.

Great objections were made in some quarters to the proposed site in Hyde Park; but as they were not raised on really public grounds, they were gradually overcome by the interest which the public at large manifested in the success of the undertaking.

In consequence of the latter recommendation in the Report which was adopted by the Royal Commissioners, the following document was published by them on March 13th, 1850, copies of which appear to have found their way into almost every corner of Europe:—

"The Committee appointed by the Royal Commission to advise on 'all matters relating to the building,' having received the sanction of the Commission, are desirous of obtaining from all parties who are disposed to assist them suggestions for the general arrangement of the buildings and premises required for this Exhibition. Upon the general form of the building in plan, the distribution of its parts, the mode of access, and the internal arrangements and contrivances, will depend the convenience and general fitness of such a building; and it is upon these points that the Committee seek information and suggestions, and wish to encourage the most extended competition in the preparation of plans. The Committee do not propose to offer any pecuniary reward for such plans—they rely upon the desire which men of all countries will feel to forward the objects of the proposed Exhibition. The Committee think it probable that, when the plans are received, they may not be limited to the selection of any one plan, but may derive useful ideas from many; and that the best plan may be determined upon by the help of this general assistance. As the credit of any such plan will be due solely to the contributors, the Committee propose to make a report, in which they will acknowledge by name those whose plans had been wholly or partially adopted, or who had afforded the most useful suggestions; and the Committee hope to be able to offer such other honorary distinction to the successful contributors as the circumstances may appear to warrant. In order to guide the contributors in the preparation of such plans and designs, and to facilitate the examination and the comparison of them when received, the Committee have enumerated concisely the principal 'desiderata' for such a building, and have laid down certain rules and conditions to which they earnestly request the contributors to conform, as the Committee will be under the necessity of abiding strictly by the regulation of not acknowledging any plans which may be sent in a form inconsistent with these rules. Copies of the engraved plan of the ground referred to may be had on application to the secretaries of the Commission, at the New Palace at Westminster."

An engraved plan of the site which had been fixed upon, together with the subjoined regulations, which all competitors would be expected to observe, were subsequently issued to all applicants:—

"1. The communications from contributors must consist of a single sheet of paper, not larger than the accompanying engraving, with a simple ground-plan upon a scale of 1·1000 of the full size, with such elevations and sections only of the building, and on the same sheet, as may be necessary to elucidate the system proposed—such elevations and sections not being intended to convey more than a general idea of the building, and not entering into details of construction or of architectural decoration—to be accompanied by a short, clear-written explanation of the system recommended, on a separate sheet. Any contributor wishing to send two designs must send separate and distinct communications, each conforming to the above conditions. No communications made inconsistent with these conditions, or any plan prepared upon a different scale from that prescribed, can be received. The plans, &c., must be sent on or before the 8th of April next, addressed to the Secretaries of the Exhibition, New Palace at Westminster, London. It is suggested that the most convenient mode of preparing the plan, elevation, and section, would be to draw them upon one of the engraved copies of the plan of the ground which accompany these instructions.—2. The building is to be erected on the space marked A B C D, and must not extend beyond the boundaries of the shaded portion. The groups of trees shown on the plan must be preserved. The principal public approaches are by the roads E F and G H. The road K L will be available only for foot-passengers. There will be no objection to the formation of cross-roads between the two last, G H and K L, if the design of the building requires it.—3. The roofed portion of the building is to cover a space of 700,000 square feet, or about 65,000 square metres; and the whole building must not occupy, including open spaces, an area of more than 900,000 square feet, or about 84,000 square metres. The building generally will be of one storey only.—4. No space will be required for cattle, or for shrubs or flowers.—5. It may be assumed, so far as it affects the ground-plan, that the light will be obtained entirely from the roof, and the building will be constructed of fire-proof materials.

"The general requirements are—simplicity of arrangement; economy of space; capability of extending or curtailing the building without destroying its symmetry as a whole, or interfering with the general arrangement, it being impossible to determine the exact extent of roof required until a late period of construction. Adaptation for the erection of separate portions of the building at different periods. Conveniences of ingress and egress, with facilities of access to all parts of the Exhibition, either from the exterior or interior. Means of classification of the various objects of different departments. Wall-space for the display of articles requiring it. Means of affording private access and accommodation for exhibitors, with counting-houses, if required. Committee-rooms, council-rooms, public re-freshment-rooms, and all other public and private accommodation. (This portion of the building may be in two or more storeys if required.) Internal arrangements, by which, under proper regulations, large crowds of visitors may circulate freely, and have convenient access to all parts of the Exhibition, and uninterrupted means of examining the various objects exhibited."

THE COMPETITION DESIGNS

HOUGH the time allowed for the preparation of drawings was but short, being only about one month, no less than 233 designs were sent in, many of them of an elaborate architectural character. Of these, thirty-eight, or one-sixth of the whole, were received from the different foreign countries of Europe (France, twenty-seven; Belgium, two; Holland, three; Hanover, one; Naples, one; Switzerland, two; Rhine Prussia, one; Hamburgh, one); 138, or more than half the entire number, from London and its vicinity, where the interest excited was naturally more immediate; fifty-one from the provincial towns of England; six from Scotland, and three from Ireland. Seven were sent anonymously. The small number contributed by the sister kingdoms seems rather remarkable.

The greater part of these designs were, of course, contributed by members of the architectural and engineering professions, but some were the productions of amateurs, and one among them purported to be the suggestion of a lady. Here, then, was matter enough not only to assist, but even, from its great variety, to perplex the Committee, since at once every possible variety of style in decoration, material in construction, and system in arrangement, were strenuously recommended by the authors of the respective designs as the great ultimatum sought for.

To Mr. Digby Wyatt, whose services were to a great extent withdrawn from the Executive Committee, in order that his professional knowledge of the subject might be placed at the disposal of the Building Committee, was intrusted the arduous task of examining and classifying these incongruous materials, and of eliminating from them such general principles of arrangement as seemed most worthy of the attentive consideration of the Committee. The result of this gentleman's minute examination was embodied in a Report, upon the basis of the recommendations contained in which the subsequent utilitarian portions of the design of the Building Committee would appear to have been founded.

After holding about fifteen protracted sittings, the Committee presented the following Report to the Royal Commission on the 9th of May:—

"**May it please your Royal Highness,**

"*My Lords and Gentlemen,*

"We have the honour to report that we have examined the numerous plans so liberally contributed by native and foreign architects in accordance with the public invitation.

"Exhausting in their numerous projects and suggestions almost every conceivable variety of building, the authors of those designs have materially assisted us in arriving at the conclusions which we have now the honour to report.

"We have been aided in our analysis of this subject by a great amount of thought and elaboration thus brought to bear upon it from various points of view.

"We have, however, arrived at the unanimous conclusion, that able and admirable as many of these designs appeared to be, there was yet no single one so accordant with the peculiar objects in view, either in the principle or detail of its arrangements, as to warrant us in recommending it for adoption.

"In some of the least successful of the designs submitted, we find indicated errors and difficulties to be avoided, whilst in the abler and more practicable of them, there are valuable conceptions and suggestions which have greatly assisted us in framing the plan we have now the honour to lay before you. In preparing this design we have been governed mainly by three considerations:—

"1. The provisional nature of the building.

"2. The advisability of constructing it as far as possible in such a form as to be available, with the least sacrifice of labour and material, for other purposes, as soon as its original one shall have been fulfilled, thus insuring a minimum ultimate cost.

"3. Extreme simplicity, demanded by the short time in which the work must be completed.

"For the arrangements of the plan we rely for effect on honesty of construction, vastness of dimension, and fitness of each part to its end.

"The principal points of excellence we have endeavoured to attain are—

"1. Economy of construction.

"2. Facilities for the reception, classification, and display of goods.

"3. Facilities for the circulation of visitors.

"4. Arrangement for grand points of view.

"5. Centralisation of supervision.

"6. Some striking feature to exemplify the present state of the science of construction in this country.

"The first of these, ECONOMY, is attained by doing away with any internal walls (all divisions being made by the necessary stalls), by reducing the whole construction, with the exception of the dome, to cast iron columns, supporting the lightest form of iron roof in long unbroken lines, and by the whole of the work being done in the simplest manner, and adapted in all respects to serve hereafter for other purposes.

"The second, facilities for the RECEPTION, CLASSIFICATION, and DISPLAY of goods. The main central entrance for the reception of objects for exhibition will probably be that most approachable from the public road. All cases accompanying goods will be examined, registered, catalogued, &c., in the offices of the Executive; the packing-cases will then be put upon a truck running on a line of rails laid down temporarily, and conveyed to the centre turn-table, from which they may be carried by a line of rails at right angles to the first, to the end of the transverse gallery, in which they may be destined to be placed.

"The most important condition to insure successful *classification* is, that those to whom the duty of arrangement may be confided should be hampered by no fixed limits of space, such as would have been the case had the building been divided into a number of halls, sections, or chambers. The plan submitted fulfils this condition perfectly; as objects can be arranged just as they are received, and moved, if necessary, from gallery to gallery with great facility.

"The successful display of the goods would be best insured by leaving, under certain general restrictions, the fitting up of each stall to the Exhibitor or his Agent, floor-space only being allotted to each; and stands, frames, brackets, shelves, &c., being put up by a contractor's carpenter, at a fixed tariff.

"The best light is provided, and the most economical wall-space is proposed to be furnished by connecting pillar to pillar transversely, on the extreme north and south sides of the building, by rods, from which draperies, &c., can be suspended.

"The third, FACILITIES FOR THE CIRCULATION OF VISITORS, is thus attained. The visitor, on arrival at the central hall, proceeds at choice to any one of the four sections. He will, most probably, desire either to follow the whole course of the section selected, or will wish to go at once to some particular class or object. He will be enabled to do either the one or the other, without interfering with the general current, by means of gates or other arrangements, which shall insure the current of visitors passing in one direction. If he desire to proceed rapidly from one end of the building to the other, and finds the great central gangway at all blocked up, he will, no doubt, be able to get on by either the north or south corridors, fifteen feet wide. Numerous doors of egress in these latter afford ready means of exit for a large number of persons. Seats are provided in the middle of the great central gangway for those who may desire to rest.

"The fourth, ARRANGEMENT FOR GRAND POINTS OF VIEW. The view from or to the centre of the building will, from its extent, be necessarily imposing. The seats and main avenues are arranged so that, on the occasion of the distribution of the prizes, an immense number of persons may be accommodated. Most interesting views might be obtained from galleries constructed at either end of the building and around the dome, for the admission of the public to which some small charge might be made.

"The fifth, CENTRALISATION OF SUPERVISION. All the business of the Exhibition will be carried on in one spot, and be readily under control. The Royal Commission, the principal Committees, Clerks, Accountants, Police, &c., would be together, and in so large an establishment it would be absolutely necessary, or much time would be wasted in walking from one point to another. Passages running behind the money-takers' boxes, with glazed doors into them, would enable each accountant to detect anything improper that might be going on, and to exchange and balance checks, money, &c., at any moment. Telegraphic communication with each of the four pay-places will permit orders to be given, cash accounts,

&c., to be issued and returned, from and to the head-accountant's office, as often as may be necessary.

"Four Committee-rooms, one for a Jury in each section, have been provided at the extreme east and west ends. The duties of such Committees being deliberative, and not executive, it is not necessary that they should be accommodated in the Central Establishment, where they would be more liable to be disturbed than at the extremity of the building.

"A policeman stationed in each gallery would, from his elevated position, be enabled to observe much which might escape detection if he mingled only with the crowd.

"The sixth, SOME STRIKING FEATURE TO EXEMPLIFY THE PRESENT STATE OF THE SCIENCE OF CONSTRUCTION IN THIS COUNTRY. In order that the building, in which England invites the whole world to display their richest productions, may afford, at least in one point, a grandeur not incommensurate with the occasion, we propose, by a dome of light sheet iron 200 feet in diameter, to produce an effect at once striking and admirable. From calculations which have been made of the cost of so grand a Hall, we have reason to expect that it may be executed for a sum not greatly exceeding the cost of the simplest form of roof likely to be adopted to cover the same area.

"It is to be borne in mind that a considerable amount of any such difference may be recovered, should this portion of the building be converted hereafter to other purposes, which is more than probable. This vast dome it is proposed to light mainly from one circle of light in its centre, and thus the sculpture will be pleasingly and suitably lit.

"Six out of the eight openings in the cylinder of the dome would be well adapted for the exhibition of stained glass windows of great extent, while the two remaining arches will open to the main central gallery. The lower part of some of the voids will admit the eye to turf and shrubs, and produce a great freshness of effect.

"The immense continuity of the Central Avenue will be broken and relieved by a variation in the roof opposite the openings to the second and third sets of refreshment-rooms, and windows for the reception of Stained Glass may be placed at the ends of each transverse gallery, thus terminating the vista for each.

"It now only remains to explain the course of action we would recommend for adoption as soon as the principles of the plan, &c., shall be positively decided.

"We consider this to be an occasion upon which the greatest amount of intellectual and commercial ingenuity and ability should be called out; and that a generous rivalry among those best fitted to execute the principal portions of this vast structure may lead to results which no amount of detailed study that we could possibly give to this matter would supply.

"We would therefore recommend that every advantage should be taken of the accumulated and experimental knowledge and resources of intelligent and enterprising contractors, and that every opportunity should be afforded to them of DISTINGUISHING THEMSELVES. We would therefore recommend as the best means of enlisting their services the following course of action:

"Adopting the approved design as a basis, we would proceed immediately to prepare such working-drawings and specifications as may be necessary, and to issue invitations for tenders to execute Works in accordance with them, requesting from competitors, in addition, such suggestions and modifications, accompanied with estimates of cost, as might possibly become the means of effecting a considerable reduction upon the general expense.

"W. Cubitt, *Chairman*."

The following Report of the Committee on the competition plans submitted, and which was so unfavourably received by the public, and more particularly by the profession, was presented to the Royal Commission on the 16th of May:—

"May it please your Royal Highness,

"My Lords and Gentlemen,

"Your Committee beg leave to report, that the invitation issued by the Commissioners, requesting information and suggestions for the general arrangement of the Building and premises required for the Exhibition of 1851, has been responded to in the most ample and satisfactory manner, both as respects the variety of useful ideas presented to their consideration, and the liberality with which many experienced and skilful men of foreign countries, no less than of our own, have contributed their valuable time to this great undertaking, thereby evincing their entire sympathy both with the great cause of Arts and Industry in which her Majesty's Commissioners have embarked, and with the arduous labours of the Directors of the undertaking.

"The Designs and Specifications transmitted to the Committee amount to the surprising number of 233, offering an aggregate of professional sacrifice of very considerable importance; for, not confining themselves to suggestions only, which were invited by the Programme, a large proportion of them are remarkable for elaboration of thought and elegance of execution.

"Penetrated with admiration and respect for these gratuitous and valuable contributions, unexampled, they believe, in the history of competition, your Committee have devoted the most careful attention to the collection of these projects, and hasten to offer those acknowledgments which are due to their merits, and to the generous motives which have led to their execution; and they trust that the public may shortly be witnesses of the effect of this very noble emulation of the skill of all countries, by the public exhibition of these designs, offering the opportunity, in the true spirit of the whole undertaking, of mutual improvement, respect, and friendship amongst the cultivators of the liberal arts in the several countries of Europe.

"It is remarkable that, while many of these contributions may be attributed to the laudable motive of professional reputation and advancement on the part of practitioners not yet sufficiently known to the public, a great number are from Gentlemen whose position in the confidence of their respective Governments or in the Republic of Arts and Letters is of the highest eminence, and who can have been actuated by no such personal motives. Already entitled to respect and admiration, they could have little to gain, while they have something to lose, in the competition for glory. The kind and frank communication, therefore, of their thoughts and experience towards this great work is to be the more highly commended. Every possible mode of accomplishing the object in view has been displayed by the respective contributors as regards economy of structure and distribution, and these qualities are united with various degrees of architectural symmetry and features in many designs. Our illustrious continental neighbours have especially distinguished themselves by compositions of the utmost taste and learning, worthy of enduring execution—examples of what might be done in the architectural illustration of the subject, when viewed in its highest aspect, and, at all events, exhibiting features of grandeur, arrangement, and grace which your Committee have not failed to appreciate.

"Amongst these several classes of design, the practical character of our own countrymen, as might have been expected, has been remarkably illustrated in some very striking and simple methods suited to the temporary purposes of the Building, due attention having been paid to the pecuniary means allotted to this part of the undertaking. The principle of suspension has been applied in a single tent of iron sheeting, covering an area averaging 2,200 feet by 400 feet by a lengthened ridge, or in separate tents on isolated supports. Others display the solution of this problem by the chapter-house principle, and a few by the umbrella or circular locomotive-engine-house system of railway-stations, either with a central column or groups of columns sustaining domes or roofs to the extent of four hundred feet diameter.

"Grandeur and simplicity of distribution are carried out with great architectural effect in other compositions, and the general arrangement by columnar supports has been also variously and elegantly developed. The system of iron roofing, with all the architectural powers of which that material is susceptible, has been adopted by some with signal enterprise, ingenuity, and power.

"In another class of design the authors have viewed with enthusiasm the great occasion and object of the proposed Exhibition, and have waived all considerations of expense. They have indulged their imaginations, and employed the resources of their genius and learning, in the composition of arrangements which present the utmost grandeur and beauty of architecture, suited to a permanent Palace of Science and Art. These, as addressed to the architectural Student, are of the highest value, reminding him of all the conditions of his art—the Egyptian hypostyle, the Roman thermæ, or of the Arabian or Saracenic inventions. And though their expense has placed them beyond reach, they cannot fail to inspire and elevate the treatment of the reality. They at all events confer great obligations on the lovers of the Fine Arts, for the authors have evidently felt that, if one of the results to be expected from the proposed Exhibition may be to prove that the simplest object of ingenuity and skill should not be devoid of some of the attractions of taste, the Building itself ought to be an illustration of that important principle.

"The Committee, however, have been unable to select any one design as combining all the requisites which various considerations render essential. But the judgment and taste evinced by a large number of the contributors have enabled the Committee to arrive more promptly at their conclusions, and they have freely availed themselves of most valuable suggestions in directing the preparation of a fresh design for the proposed building.

"They have consequently been most earnest in the desire to fulfil the just expectations of the various competitors, and feel assured that your Royal Highness and the Commission will be of opinion that the most unreserved and handsome acknowledgments are due to those able men of science and art who have in so disinterested a manner submitted such admirable projects for the consideration and assistance of the Committee. They beg, therefore, to submit, as their opinion, that the following gentlemen are entitled to honourable and favourable mention, on account of architectural merit, ingenious construction or disposition, or for graceful arrangement of plan.

"And they cannot conclude without calling attention to the designs, accompanied by models, of M. Hector Horeau, Architect of Paris, and of Messrs. Turner, of Dublin, as evincing most daring and ingenious disposition and construction.[1]

"W. Cubitt, *Chairman*."

Some of the strongest objections to this Report are very fairly urged in a letter which appeared in the *Builder* of the 15th of June, a part of which is subjoined:—

"Part II. of the Report contains what I suppose is to be taken as the best exposition of the merits of contributors that the Committee can give, which commences by stating, in a tone of commendation, that, 'not confining themselves to SUGGESTIONS ONLY, which were invited by the PROGRAMME, a large proportion of them are remarkable for elaboration of thought and elegance of execution.' This, I would contend, is clearly a breach of the specified conditions, viz., that SUGGESTIONS ONLY were to be given—that the plan or drawing sent in was to be A MERE OUTLINE SKETCH, upon a SINGLE SHEET; and the Committee even recommended that it would be most convenient merely to trace it upon the common paper on which the 'plan of site' was supplied to the public, a space being left upon the sheet for SKETCHING any sections or elevations that might be necessary to illustrate the design; and that a written description, limited also to 'a single sheet,' was all the exposition of their ideas that authors would be allowed to give. The Report goes on to state, that 'our illustrious continental neighbours have especially distinguished themselves [in designing a temporary building for an exhibition] by compositions of the utmost taste and learning, worthy of enduring execution—examples of what might be done in the ARCHITECTURAL illustration of the subject [the conditions strictly enjoined contributors not to enter into architectural detail] when viewed in its highest aspect, and, at all events, exhibiting features of grandeur, arrangement, and grace which your Committee have not failed to appreciate.' It then places in contradistinction to these no doubt admirable but out-of-place productions of architectural genius, the 'practical character of the de-

---

[1] A complete list of the names of all the competitors, together with those selected by the Committee, will be found in the Appendix; also a description and views of the two designs specially referred to.

signs of our own countrymen,' which it states, 'as might have been expected, has been remarkably illustrated in some very striking and simple methods, suited to the temporary purposes of the building, due attention having been paid by them to the pecuniary means allotted to this part of the undertaking.' Yet, notwithstanding this comparison, clearly and indisputably in favour of our own countrymen, as regards the object sought and the conditions stipulated by the Committee, we find by the selected list of those authors who are to receive 'the highest honorary distinction' the Commissioners can award, that the Committee can only discover, out of 195 English and 38 foreign contributors, THREE Englishmen entitled to reward, the remaining FIFTEEN out of the eighteen selected being foreigners; or, as regards the whole numbers, in proportion of 1 to 65 of 'our own countrymen,' the authors of the 'striking and simple,' so admirably 'suited to the temporary purpose of the building,' and 1 to about 2½ of foreigners, who, in designing for a temporary building, to be simple, cheap, and readily constructed, have so over-shot the mark as to produce 'compositions' commendable only for the 'utmost taste and learning, and worthy of enduring execution.' Surely something must be wrong here, either the Report or the selected list—possibly both.

"In conclusion, I cannot help avowing the opinion that a wrong, though I believe unintentionally, has been done to many of the 233 who so readily and 'generously' responded to the call for their ideas; more particularly as I know, from personal inspection, that at least ONE of the plans altogether omitted from the Report contains FIVE of the leading features of the approved design."

But to judge of this matter fairly, it must be mentioned that, although the number of foreign competitors was small, the majority of them were men already well known for their talents and professional skill; in all cases their designs evinced considerable study of the subject (both architecturally and in a practical point of view), and manifested a desire to exhibit to English professional men the proficiency of their continental brethren. On the other hand, many of the designs from the competitors at home were much slighter suggestions presented in a less elaborate form. Under these circumstances, it is not to be wondered at that those eminent men of the technical professions who, on this occasion, came forward with practical suggestions for the assistance of the Committee, and designs calculated rather to assist with thoughts than to charm by the graces of elegant drawing or symmetrical disposition, should seem to have been found wanting in this first trial with all the world. It should further be borne in mind, that the nature of competitions is not so well understood in some foreign countries, where they are of less frequent occurrence, than with us. It must at the same time be admitted that the practice of disregarding and exceeding the instructions in competitions is too much a matter of general complaint in England to be brought forward as a new grievance against our continental brethren.

After the publication of the above Report, the competition designs were all exhibited in the rooms of the Institution of Civil Engineers, in Great George-street, which were liberally placed at the disposal of the Committee for this purpose; and of those who visited this interesting exhibition, many, no doubt, must have sympathised with those feelings which dictated the decision of the Committee.

From an attentive examination of these designs, presenting the subject in such exceedingly varied forms, one of the peculiar difficulties of the case becomes apparent, namely, the total absence of any precedent to guide or afford suggestions to the designer; for the small number of buildings erected or adapted for a similar purpose have been on so limited a scale that their example could not afford much assistance in designing a structure to meet all the requirements of the present case. This building differed from all previous ones in being intended to accommodate the products of all nations, instead of being confined to those of one only; in which case the arrangement would have been more certain and more readily provided for.

BUILDINGS USED FOR PREVIOUS EXHIBITIONS IN FRANCE, GERMANY, AND ENGLAND

S a comparison of some of these earlier buildings with the first erected in London for a similar purpose cannot fail to be interesting, a short notice of them may not be deemed out of place. The most important amongst them are those temporary structures which have been erected in Paris for the periodical Industrial Expositions, with reference to the last of which we cannot do better than quote, from Mr. Digby Wyatt's instructive and masterly Report, that part where the building is treated of:—

"The vast edifice which has been erected to contain the specimens of manufacture selected for exhibition in the year 1849 is situated on the same site as that occupied by a similar building in the year 1844. The Carré de Marigny, on which it has been placed, is a large oblong piece of ground, abutting on the main avenue of the Champs Elysées, and as a site offers every possible advantage, being of a gravelly soil, already efficiently drained, and standing on the line of a continually moving series of public conveyances. The Champs Elysées, though at some considerable distance from the great centre of Parisian population, are still so universal a place of resort, that they may be fairly assumed to be "in the way" of even the poorest classes of the community. The elevation may be admirably seen from all the approaches to the building, and it has the advantage of being in immediate proximity to the residence of the President of the Republic.

PLAN OF THE BUILDING FOR THE FRENCH EXPOSITION IN 1849.

1. Cattle-shed.	5. Productions of	08. Principal Entrance.
2. Machinery.	Parisian Industry.	09. Guard-house.
3. Chemical Products.	6. Horticulture.	10. Fountain.
4. Metal Works.	7. Woven Goods.	11. Reservoir of Rain Water.

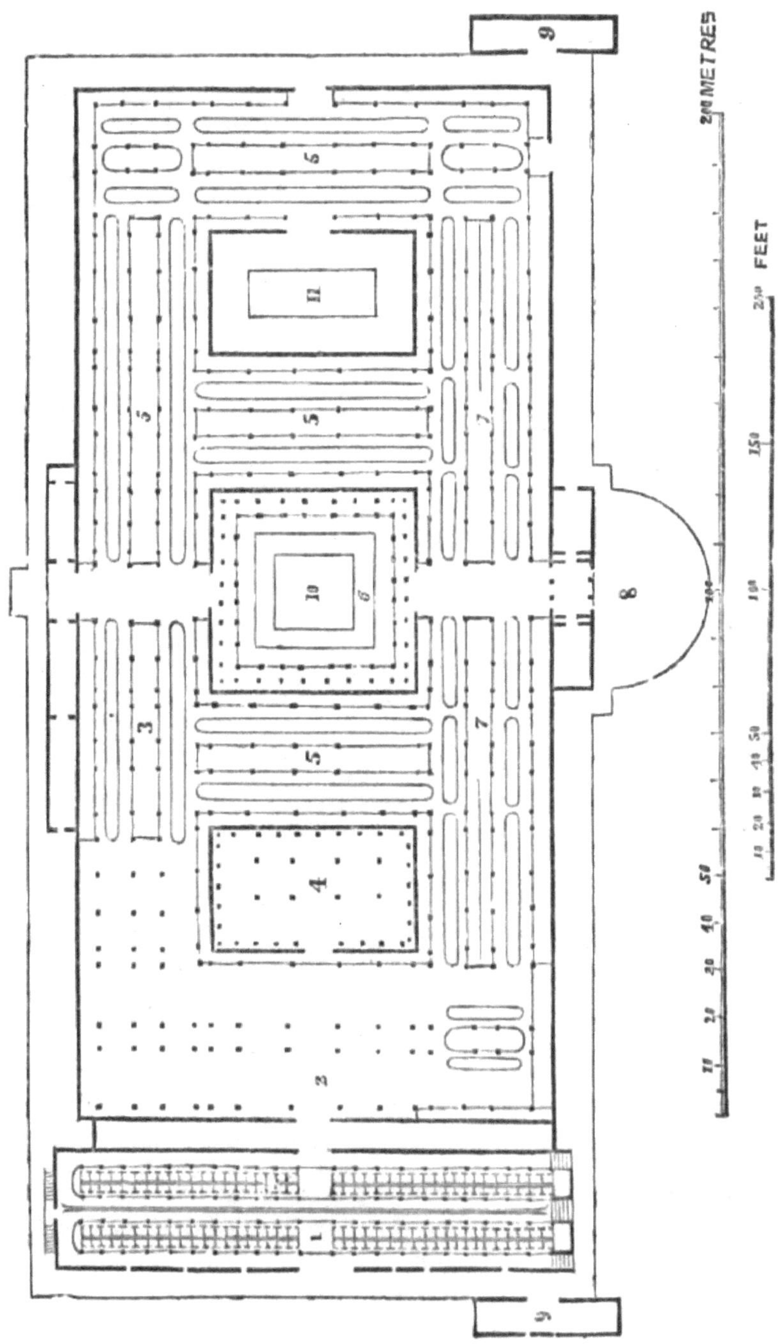
METRES
FEET

VIEW OF THE PRINCIPAL ENTRANCE.

"The whole plot of the present building (exclusive of the agricultural department) covers a vast parallelogram of 206 metres by 100 (about 675 by 328 feet English), round the outline of which runs a gallery about 90 feet wide, divided into two avenues by a double range of pilasters. In the centre of each avenue is a set of stalls, placed back to back, for the exhibition of merchandise; and both between the central pilasters, and round, and upon the walls, other objects are placed, so that on traversing either of the four gangways (each about ten feet wide) the public have upon their right and left hands objects for inspection. In the part of the building appropriated to large machinery, of course this system cannot be carried out with the same regularity. The vast parallelogram, inclosed by a somewhat similar gallery in the year 1844, was left as one magnificent hall, within which were placed the most important objects; in the present building we find it divided by two transverse galleries, similarly arranged to those we have described, forming three court-yards; the central one being about 140 feet square, and the two lateral ones 80 feet by 140. The central court-yard is open to the sky; in the middle rises an elegant fountain placed on a platform of turf, and around are disposed sheds for the exhibition of flowers and horticultural ornaments and implements. One of the lateral courts (inclosed) receives a large collection of objects in metal-work, cast-iron, &c., and the other contains an immense reservoir, in which all the drainage from the roofs is collected, so as to form a supply of water immediately serviceable in case of fire. In addition to this great building, which corresponds with that previously erected, there is this year constructed a vast shed for the exhibition of agricultural produce and stock. It extends to a length rather greater than the width of the great parallelogram, and is about 100 feet (English) wide. Its construction is ruder than that of the 'Palace,' but it is not on that account less effective. It appears to have been originally contemplated to fill the whole of this gigantic hall with cattle, &c., and to place the agricultural implements in a long narrow gallery intervening between it and the main building; but as the stock of animals forwarded for exhibition has not proved so large as was anticipated, it has been half-filled with semi-agricultural machines, and the whole of the long narrow gallery alluded to crammed with stoves, and miscellaneous domestic mechanism.

"The whole of the building is constructed of wood, the roofs being covered with zinc: of the latter material 400,000 kilogrammes, equal to nearly 4,000 tons, are stated to have been used; and of the former, nearly 45,000 pieces of timber.

"It is hoped that the accompanying plan and views will convey a tolerably good idea both of the exterior and interior arrangements of the Exhibition. They will serve to show, at least, that a somewhat unnecessary expenditure has been gone into, and to manifest the possibility of constructing a much more simple building, possessing all the advantages of this one, at a far less cost.

"Both externally and internally there is a good deal of tasteless and unprofitable ornament; all the pilasters are papered and painted in a species of graining to imitate light oak, and even the ceiling is covered over with the same work. Large 'carton pierre' trusses apparently support the timbers, and a painted bronze bas-relief fills the tympanum of the pediment, at the principal entrance. The architecture of the whole is 'mesquin,' although the gigantic scale of the building necessarily elevates the general effect into something of impressiveness; not, however, to nearly the extent which the same outlay might have produced."

INTERIOR VIEW OF THE "PALACE."

Mr. Wyatt further states that the total cost of this building was about 450,000 francs, or about 18,000*l.*, which, however, he considers was an unnecessarily large outlay. He mentions, also, that the building erected on the previous occasion, in 1844, was in some respects more suitable for the purpose, especially from its greater simplicity of arrangement, a remark it will be well to bear in mind in considering the various designs for the building in Hyde Park. The accompanying plates will enable the reader readily to follow all the details of the description.

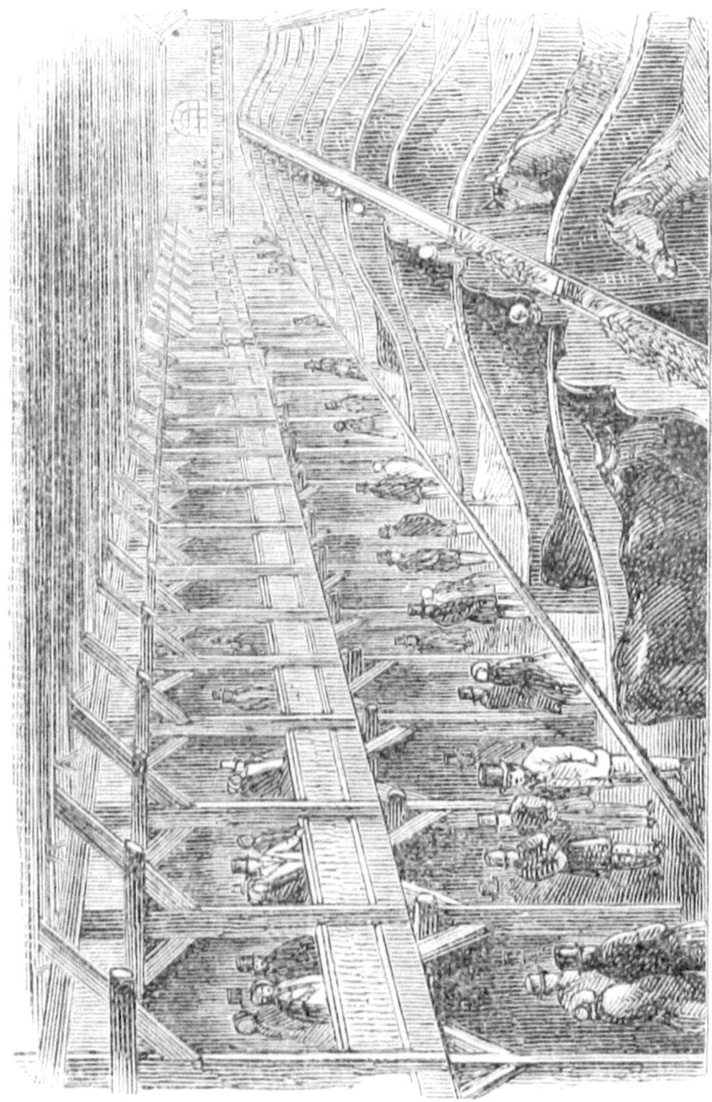

INTERIOR OF THE CATTLE-SHED.

The permanent building erected by the King of Bavaria at Munich, likewise for periodical Exhibitions, is on a much smaller scale than those in Paris, and must be regarded rather as having afforded an opportunity for that manifestation of architectural display in public buildings for which its Royal projector was so well known, than as being peculiarly fitted for its purpose. It is divided internally into various halls for the different classes of objects; but as the proportion of these must necessarily vary at every Exhibition, such an arrangement cannot be deemed the most suitable for the purpose.

At Berlin, where several Industrial Exhibitions have taken place, no distinct building has been provided, but some already existing one has been temporarily adapted and fitted up for the purpose; thus, on the last occasion, Kroll's WINTERGARTEN, a large establishment for public amusement, which has been recently destroyed by fire, was made use of. The large central saloon, with the smaller ones flanking it, forming, in fact, one space 310 feet long, and 82 feet broad at the widest point, afforded a very good opportunity for the arrangement of the objects to be exhibited, some of which were placed in the gallery of the large saloon.

On a previous occasion a part of the Royal Arsenal building was appropriated, and the Exhibition embraced two storeys.

In our own country, exhibitions of manufactures have taken place in several of the most important towns, generally in spaces only temporarily adapted; but in 1849 the first building in this country intended solely for the purpose of an exhibition of manufactures was erected at Birmingham, on the occasion of the meeting of the British Association in that town.

The building alluded to included a space extending to 10,000 square feet, and a corridor, giving additional accommodation of 800 square feet, connected the temporary exhibition-room with Bingley-house, within the grounds of which the building was erected; and including the rooms of the old mansion, the total area covered by the Exhibition was equal to 12,800 feet, or only about one-seventeenth of the area covered by the last building erected in the Champs Elysées. The cost of this building was about 1,300*l*. It was opened to the public on the 3rd of September, 1849.

In most of the buildings alluded to above, the principal defect seemed to be that a definite and fixed subdivision of space was made for a classification of objects which was necessarily uncertain. This appears to have determined the Committee in the arrangement of the plan which they presented in a general form to the Royal Commission at the same time with the Report already quoted; and although the design was slightly modified during the progress of the working-drawings subsequently made, this is, perhaps, the best place for introducing a description of it.

VIEW OF KROLL'S WINTERGARTEN AT BERLIN.

PLAN OF KROLL'S WINTERGARTEN, BERLIN.

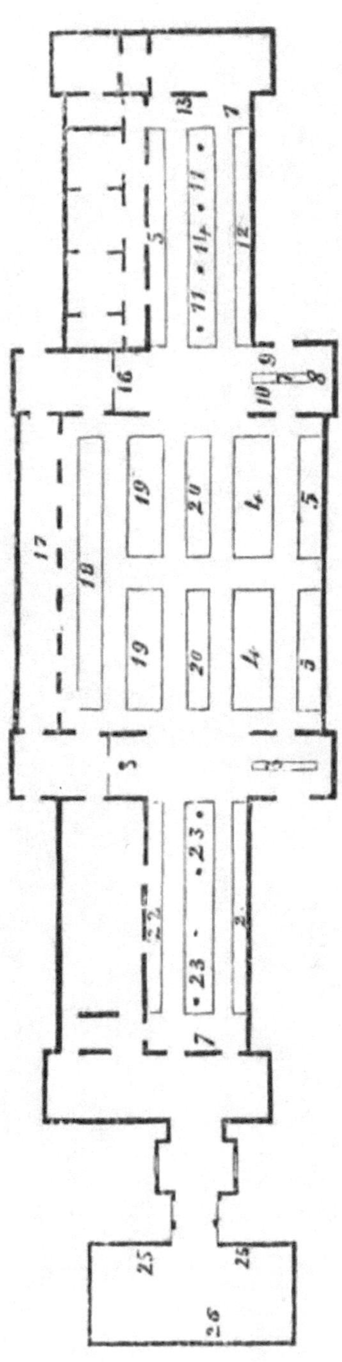

1. Electric Telegraph.
2. Chemical Products.
3. Porcelain and Bronzes.
4. Machinery.
5. Hardware.
6. Zinc Works.
7. Plate and Jewellery.
8. Lithography.
9. Watches, &c.
10. Cutlery.
11. Scientific Instruments.
12. Bookbinding.
13. Embroidery.
14. Ornamental Blinds.
15. Silks and Velvets.
16. Furs.
17. Pianofortes.
18. Carriages.
19. Furniture.
20. Lamps, &c.
21. Turned Articles.
22. Woollen Fabrics.
23. Leather Articles.
24. Hats & Felt Articles.
25. Machinery.
26. Carriages.

VIEW OF THE BIRMINGHAM EXPOSITION BUILDING.

It has been already mentioned that at the time the Committee received the competition designs, they obtained the assistance of Mr. Digby Wyatt, the secretary to the Executive Committee, to aid them in the preparation of drawings, although Mr. Scott Russell officially filled the post of secretary to the Building Committee. At a somewhat later stage of the Committee's proceedings, when the general design for the proposed building had been approved by the Royal Commission, and it became necessary to prepare working drawings for the same with extraordinary despatch, Mr. Charles Heard Wild, as engineer, and Mr. Owen Jones, as architect, were appointed to co-operate with Mr. Wyatt in carrying out this object.

DESCRIPTION OF THE BUILDING COMMIT-TEE'S DESIGN

HE site to have been occupied by the building designed by the Committee was the same as that on which the building has been actually erected, namely between Rotten-row and the drive in Hyde Park, but the area proposed to be covered was somewhat larger, the length of the building being about 2,200 feet, and the greatest width nearly 450 feet. The central space was occupied by an immense rotunda 200 feet in diameter, the cupola rising to a height of more than 160 feet, and exceeding the span of that of St. Peter's at Rome by 61 feet, and of St. Paul's in London by 88 feet. The dome for covering this rotunda consisted of wrought-iron ribs, supporting a covering of corrugated iron, the whole resting on a wall or drum of brickwork, about 60 feet high; a large opening in the centre was to be glazed for the admission of light.

This large open area was intended for the exhibition of groups of sculpture, fountains, and other objects requiring great space in order to be seen to advantage; at the same time the cupola would have presented a striking instance of the constructive skill of this country.

The remaining area of the building was divided into avenues 48 feet wide, by iron columns 24 feet apart, this dimension having been determined on as that most likely to work in well for the division of the counters and passages. One of the 48-feet avenues on the main axis of the building was spanned by semicircular ribs of wrought iron supporting the roof, which rose here to a greater height than the rest of the building; the other avenues were covered with roofing very similar to that commonly seen in railway-sheds, the whole being rendered as light as possible, and constructed in iron covered with slating; the light being in all cases admitted by a range of sky-lights at the apex of the roof, which was also adapted for ventilation. The height of the main avenue was 52 feet, and of the others 36 feet, from the floor throughout. A corridor of communication 15 feet wide was carried round the whole of the building, interrupted only by the open courts; this, with the main avenue, afforded the visitor to the Exhibition the means of reaching any particular point without threading a maze of small passages. The inclosing walls were to be of brick, relieved externally by panels in two colours; but there were to be no internal division walls except those necessary to surround the various courts which were left on account of the trees.

The executive offices were grouped on either side of the principal entrance, which was placed immediately opposite Prince's Gate; and at this, as well as at the entrances at either end and on the north front, large arched recesses were introduced which served as vestibules, and formed at the same time prominent and striking features to relieve the necessarily monotonous aspect of the building. Along the whole of the principal front and at the ends of the building a pent or overhanging roof projected about 15 feet, to enable visitors in bad weather to be set down under cover, and the exit-doors, of which there were altogether 24, were further protected by porches.

The water was to be conveyed from the roof through the columns which supported it, and which were for this purpose connected with the necessary drain-pipes, &c.

Very ample accommodation was provided for refreshments in the open courts which were necessarily left for the preservation of the trees, particularly in that at the western end of the building, where there was proposed to be placed a large establishment, comprising two storeys, with somewhat the arrangement of the French cafés, including a fine saloon on the first floor, upwards of thirty feet wide and nearly one hundred feet long; separate spaces were also provided for the accommodation of exhibitors. This was the only part of the building, with the exception of the executive offices, which was to have an upper storey.

An objection might, perhaps, be raised to this part of the building, that it was too commodious, and that there might be some danger of its being converted into a lounge, while it was occupying too much of the space intended for the Exhibition, for a secondary, though certainly necessary purpose; it was, however, considered by the Committee, that of the vast number of visitors that might be expected to be in the building at one time, so many would avail themselves of the accommodation provided as to render a less amount undesirable. The principal courts were surrounded by a covered way, where refreshments were also to be served at long counters, in the manner of the railway-stations.

All these arrangements will readily be understood by a reference to the plan of the design we have been describing, which plan, together with a view taken from the south-east angle of the building, will place before the reader the result of the labours of the Committee. The materials proposed for the construction of this building were fire-proof throughout, with the exception of the floor and its supporting timbers.

GROUND PLAN OF THE BUILDING COMMITTEE'S DESIGN.

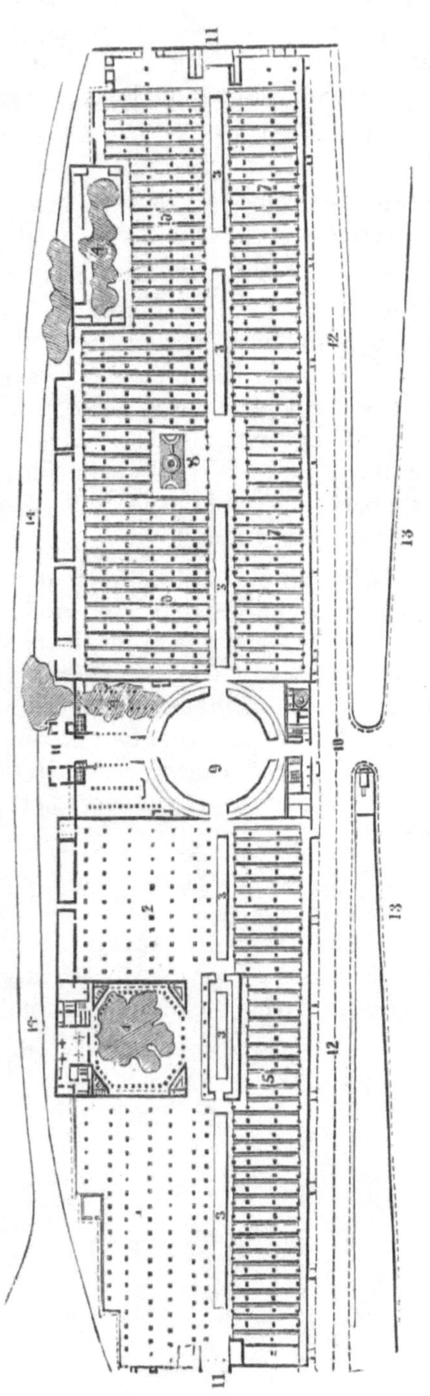

1. Machinery in Motion.

2. Other Machinery.

3. Seats for Visitors.

4. Refreshment Courts.

5. Raw Materials.

6. Manufactures.

7. Sculpture and the Plastic Arts.

8. Small Court.

09. The Rotunda.

10. Principal Entrance and Executive Offices.

11. The Other Entrances.

12. The Drive in the Park.

13. The Kensington Road.

14. The Queen's Private Road.

The above design, at least in all its leading features, for some of the details were subsequently added, was laid before the Royal Commission, at the same time with the Report already quoted, and was by them approved, and the Committee proceeded to prepare the necessary working-drawings and specifications for the execution of the work. These proceedings of the Committee occupied until the 24th of June, when large lithographed copies of the most important of the drawings, together with printed copies of the specifications and other details, were issued from the offices of the Executive, contractors having been some time previously invited by public advertisement to send in tenders for the execution of either a part or the whole of the work. The tenders were to be on two systems, one on the supposition that the Royal Commission were to become the *bona fide* purchasers of the building; the other, that the contractors were to erect and maintain the building during the time of the Exhibition, after which they were to remove it and take back the materials at their own risk, receiving a proportionably diminished sum.

It has been considered necessary to describe thus minutely the labours of the Committee and the design in which they resulted, in order to show how far it paved the way for that which was subsequently adopted, and to give them that credit which they undoubtedly deserve for devoting so much of their valuable time for the furtherance of a great public undertaking.

OPPOSITION TO THIS DESIGN

HE design of the Building Committee, when published to the world, met with anything but public approbation; some of the objectors called in question the practicability of the execution of the enormous dome, at least within the time assigned; others complained that the outlay would be unnecessarily large for a purpose avowedly temporary, and expressed their fears that so costly a structure once erected, there would be the less probability of its subsequent removal; but the objection which appeared to have most weight with the public at large was, the great amount of solid brick construction in the walls, &c., which, it was urged, would require a longer time than could be allowed for their erection, and that the carting of the materials would cause serious injury in the Park and the surrounding neighbourhood. This strong current of objection seemed to bid fair to overwhelm the much-abused design. To increase the difficulties which seemed to gather round the progress of this noble undertaking, an exceedingly vexatious and factious agitation was got up in opposition to the proposed site in Hyde Park, and petitions and counter-petitions were presented to both Houses of Parliament, and much of the time of the Legislature was wasted in fruitless discussion on the subject. The Building Committee thought it desirable, under these circumstances, to lay before the public their reasons for recommending the site in the Park, and therefore issued a memorandum of the grounds on which it had been selected.[2] The result was, that the opposition was defeated in the Legislature, and finally crushed by the force of public opinion.

---

[2] This "memorandum" will be found in the Appendix.

THE TENDERS

N the mean time the competing contractors had been obliged to strain every nerve to get their tenders ready by the 10th of July, when, altogether, nineteen were sent in, but eight only were for undertaking the whole of the work; the amounts of these are stated to have ranged between 150,000*l.* and 120,000*l.*, and this for the use only of the materials for the building. But, at the same time, in accordance with the recommendation and invitation contained in the last part of the Report already quoted, Messrs. Fox, Henderson and Co. presented a tender upon a design entirely different in construction and appearance, though resembling that of the Committee in the general arrangement of the plan.

This design was by Mr. Joseph Paxton, and resembled in its general form the building as it is now executed, with the exception of the transept and semicircular roof, which were subsequently added, and were suggested by Mr. Barry.

The result of the tenders appears to have been unfavourable to the Committee's design; and in their Report to the Royal Commission on the subject, made a few days afterwards, they proposed to omit the great dome and some portions of the design which were not essential, by which they considered that the cost of its execution might be reduced below 100,000*l.*; at the same time, they made special mention of Mr. Paxton's design, which, however, they considered would prove more expensive.

Mr. Paxton's design had been brought before the public before this period; for, considering that his best road to success would be to get a favourable verdict from that many-headed jury, he published a view and description of it in the *Illustrated News*, and, through the influence of Mr. Stephenson, he got his plans laid before the Royal Commission, in consequence of which he obtained an interview with his Royal Highness the President. The encouragement given him by the attention bestowed upon his design by the Royal Commission, and the favourable opinion of the public, had determined him to procure a tender for the execution of the work, to be sent in with those upon the Committee's design. This he was enabled to do by the great energy and promptitude of the contractors, Messrs. Fox and Henderson, to whom he applied at the eleventh hour. The difficulties that had to be overcome, owing to the shortness of the time remaining for the estimates to be made up, can scarcely be better laid before the reader than they have been by an able writer in "Household Words:" —

EXTERIOR VIEW OF THE BUILDING COMMITTEE'S DESIGN.

"It was now Saturday, and only a few days more were allowed for receiving tenders. Yet before an approximate estimate of expense could be formed, the great glass-manufacturers and iron-masters of the north had to be consulted. This happened to be *dies mirabilis* the third; for it was the identical Saturday on which the Sunday postal question had reached its crisis, and there was to be no delivery the next day! But in a country of electric telegraphs, and of indomitable energy, time and difficulties are annihilated; and it is not the least of the marvels wrought in connexion with the great edifice that, by aid of railway-parcels and the electric telegraph, not only did all the gentlemen summoned out of Warwickshire and Staffordshire appear on Monday morning at Messrs. Fox and Henderson's office, in Spring Gardens, London, to contribute their several estimates to the tender for the whole, but within a week the contractors had prepared every detailed working-drawing, and had calculated the cost of every pound of iron, of every inch of wood, and of every pane of glass.

"There is no one circumstance in the history of the manufacturing enterprise of the English nation which places in so strong a light as this its boundless resources in materials, to say nothing of the arithmetical skill in computing at what cost and in how short a time those materials could be converted to a special purpose. What was done in those few days? Two parties in London, relying on the accuracy and good faith of certain iron-masters, glass-workers in the provinces, and of one master-carpenter in London, bound themselves for a certain sum of money, and in the course of some four months, to cover eighteen acres of ground with a building upwards of a third of a mile long, and some four hundred and fifty feet broad. In order to do this, the glass-maker promised to supply, in the required time, nine hundred thousand square feet of glass (weighing more than four hundred tons), in separate panes, and these the largest that ever were made of sheet glass; each being forty-nine inches long. The iron-master passed his word in like manner to cast in due time three thousand three hundred iron columns, varying from fourteen feet and a half to twenty feet in length: thirty-four miles of guttering-tube, to join every individual column together under the ground; two thousand two hundred and twenty-four girders (but some of these are of wrought iron); besides eleven hundred and twenty-eight bearers for supporting galleries. The carpenter undertook to get ready within the specified period two hundred and five MILES of sash-bar, flooring for an area of thirty-three millions of cubic feet, besides enormous quantities of wooden walling, louvre-work, and partition.[3]

"It is not till we reflect on the vast sums of money involved in transactions of this magnitude that we can form even a slight notion of the great, almost ruinous loss, a trifling arithmetical error would have occasioned, and of the boundless confidence the parties must have had in their resources and in the correctness of their computations. Nevertheless, it was one great merit in Mr. Paxton's original details of measurement that they were contrived to facilitate calculation.

"There was little time for consideration, or for setting right a single mistake, were it ever so disastrous. On the prescribed day the tender was presented, with whatever imperfections it might have had, duly and irredeemably sealed. But af-

---

[3] The figures quoted are not quite correct, as will be seen hereafter.

ter-checkings have divulged no material error."

The Royal Commission appear from the first to have been favourably impressed with Mr. Paxton's design, partly, no doubt, because its adoption would at once silence the great bricks-and-mortar objection to the occupation of the site in Hyde Park; and the result was that, on the 16th of July, Messrs. Fox and Henderson's tender of 79,800*l.* for Mr. Paxton's design was verbally accepted, and, as soon as the necessary arrangements could be made, the contract was formally concluded.

HISTORY OF MR. PAXTON'S DESIGN

S Mr. Paxton himself has stated, the design for a building of such magnitude could not have been produced in so short a space of time without the aid of the experience he had gained in constructing other great buildings of a somewhat similar character; the progress of this experience Mr. Paxton has described in the lecture he delivered to the Society of Arts on the 13th of November, 1850, from which we have made the following extracts; and we hope to be excused by the reader for their copiousness, on the ground that no man can so well relate his own doings as the actor himself:—

"The Great Industrial Building now in the course of erection, and which forms the subject of the present paper, was not the production of a momentary consideration of the subject. Its peculiar construction, in cast-iron and glass, together with the manner of forming the vast roof, is the result of much experience in the erection of buildings of a similar kind, although on a smaller scale, which has gradually developed itself through a series of years. It may not, therefore, be uninteresting to give a brief account of the reasons which led me to investigate the subject of glass roofs and glass structures generally, and which have resulted in the Exhibition Building.

"In 1828, when I first turned my attention to the building and improvement of glass structures, the various forcing-houses at Chatsworth, as at other places, were formed of coarse thick glass and heavy woodwork, which rendered the roofs dark and gloomy, and, on this account, very ill suited for the purposes they were intended to answer. My first object was to remove this evil, and, in order to accomplish it, I lightened the rafters and sash-bars, by bevelling off their sides; and some houses which were afterwards built in this manner proved very satisfactory. I also at this time contrived a light sash-bar, having a groove for the reception of the glass; this groove completely obviated a disadvantage connected with the old mode of glazing, namely, the putty becoming continually displaced by sun, frost, and rain, after the sashes had been made for a short time, and the wet by this means finding its way betwixt the glass and the wood, and producing a continual drip in rainy weather.

"About this period the desire for metallic roofs began to extend in every direction; and as such structures had a light and graceful appearance, it became a question of importance as to the propriety of using metal sashes and rafters, instead of wooden ones, for horticultural purposes. After carefully observing the effects of those built by various persons, it became apparent to me that the expansion and contraction of metal would always militate against its general adoption, as at no season of the year could the sashes and rafters be made to fit.

"The extra expense, also, of erecting metallic-roofed houses was a consideration. In 1833 I contemplated building a new range of hot-houses; and being desirous of knowing how much they would cost, if erected of metal, a plan of the range was prepared and sent to Birmingham, and another to Sheffield, with a desire to be furnished with estimates for that purpose. The estimate from Birmingham was 1,800*l.*; and the other, from Sheffield, was 1,850*l.* These appeared to me such enormous sums, that I at once set about calculating how much the range would cost if built of wood under my own inspection; and the result was, that I was able to complete the whole range, including masonry (which was omitted in the metal estimates), for less than 500*l.*

"Besides the extra cost of metallic roofs, we must add the extreme heat of such houses in hot weather, and their coldness in times of frost; the liability to breakage of glass from expansion and contraction of the metal; the very limited duration of the smaller portions, as sash-bars, from corrosion, by exposure to the alternations of heat, cold, and moisture, inseparable from gardening operations, and which could only be prevented by making use of the expensive material, COPPER; and the difficulty, when compared with wood, of repairing any damages, as a wooden roof could at any time be set to rights by a common carpenter. These different items formed in my mind so many objections to its use, and the same disadvantages soon became generally apparent.

"It was now thought advisable by some parties that, in order to obviate the many disadvantages in the use of metal, the rafters and frame-work of the sashes ought to be made of wood, and the sash-bars of metal. This plan certainly presented more advantages than the other, yet it was quite obvious that materials so incongruous could never give satisfaction; and accordingly, in a few years, as I had anticipated, the rage for these structures gradually subsided, and the use of wood again became resorted to by most persons, as the best material for horticultural purposes.

"In the construction of glass-houses requiring much light, there always appeared to me one important objection, which no person seemed to have taken up or obviated; it was this. In plain lean-to or shed roofs, the morning and evening sun, which is on many accounts of the greatest importance in forcing fruits, presented its direct rays at a low angle, and, consequently, very obliquely to the glass. At those periods most of the rays of light and heat were obstructed by the position of the glass and heavy rafters, so that a considerable portion of time was lost both morning and evening; it consequently became evident that a system by which the glass would be more at right angles to the morning and evening rays of the sun would obviate the difficulty, and remove the obstruction to rays of light entering the house at an early and late hour of the day.

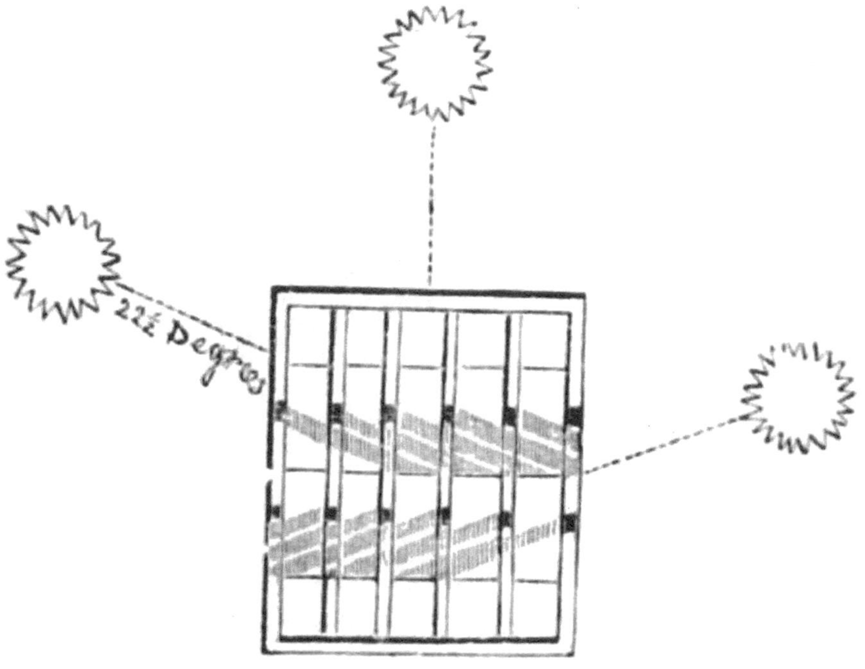

COMMON MODE OF GLAZING ROOFS.

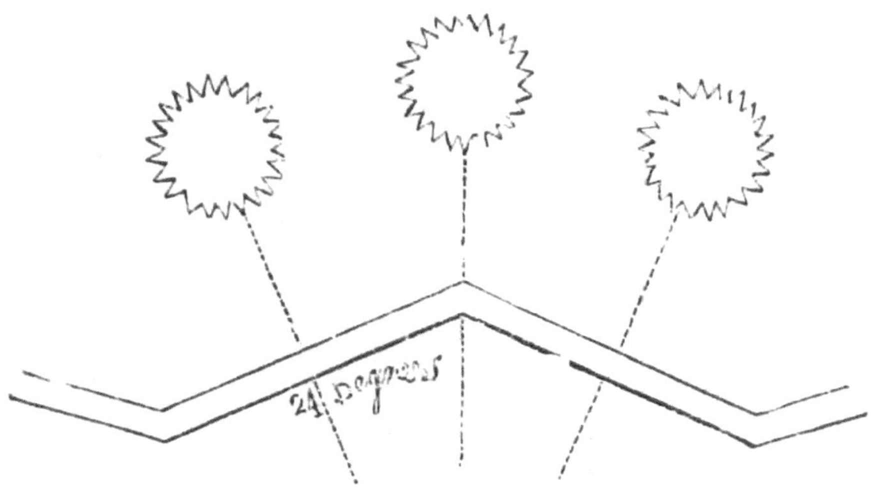

METHOD BY RIDGE-AND-FURROW.

"This led me to the adoption of the ridge-and-furrow principle for glass roofs, which places the glass in such a position that the rays of light in the mornings and evenings enter the house without obstruction, and present themselves more perpendicularly to the glass at those times when they are the least powerful; whereas at mid-day, when they are most powerful, they present themselves more obliquely to the glass. Having had this principle fixed in my mind, and being convinced of its importance, I constructed a pine-house in 1833 as an experiment, which still exists unimpaired, and has been found fully to answer the purpose.

"In 1834 I resolved to try a further experiment on a larger scale, on the ridge-and-furrow principle, in the construction of a green-house of considerable dimensions, which also remains and answers admirably. For this building I made a still lighter sash-bar than any I had previously used; on which account the house, when completed (although possessing all the advantages of wood), was as light as if constructed of metal. The whole length of this structure is 97½ feet, and its breadth 26 feet; the height at the back is 16 feet 9 inches, and in the front 12 feet 3 inches. A span so large as 26 feet could not be safely covered with a roof constructed in the ordinary way, unless the sash-bars were stronger, and the assistance of heavy rafters and numerous supports was afforded. The house presents a neat and light appearance, and consists of 15 bays, and pediments in front, supported by 16 slender reeded cast-iron columns. Whilst it makes an admirable green-house, it is also an economical building; for, at the period of its construction, notwithstanding the heavy tax on glass (since removed), it only cost at the rate of twopence and a fraction per cubic foot. At the present time, considering the change in the price of material, and the removal of the glass-tax, it could be constructed at a considerably smaller amount.

"Having in contemplation the erection of the Great Conservatory in its present form, it was determined, in 1836, to erect a new curvilinear hot-house 60 feet in length and 26 feet in width, with the elliptical roof on the ridge-and-furrow principle, to be constructed entirely of wood, for the purpose of exhibiting how roofs of this kind could be supported. The plan adopted was this: the curved rafters were composed of several boards securely nailed together on templets of wood cut to the exact curve; by this means a strength and firmness were obtained sufficient to support an enormous weight.

"In 1837 the foundations of the Great Conservatory were commenced; and in constructing so great a building it was found desirable to contrive some means for abridging the great amount of manual labour that would be required in making the immense number of sash-bars requisite for the purpose. Accordingly, I visited all the great workshops in London, Manchester, and Birmingham, to see if anything had been invented that would afford the facilities I required. The only apparatus met with was a grooving-machine, which I had at once connected with a steam-engine at Chatsworth, and which was subsequently so improved as to make the sash-bar complete.

"For this apparatus the Society of Arts, in April, 1841, awarded me a medal; and this machine is the type from which all the sash-bar machines found in use throughout the country at the present time are taken. As the Conservatory was erected under my own immediate superintendence, I am able to speak accurately as to the advantages of the machine: it has, in regard to that building alone, saved in expenses 1,400*l.* The length of each of the bars of the Conservatory is 48 inches;

only one inch shorter than those of the Exhibition Building. The machine was first used in its present form in August, 1838; and its original cost, including table, wheels, and everything complete, was 20*l.* The motive power is from a steam-engine employed on the premises for other purposes; and any well-seasoned timber may be used. The attendants required are only a man and a boy, and the expense of the power required for it when in use is comparatively trifling. The sash-bars may be made of any form, by changing the character of the saws.

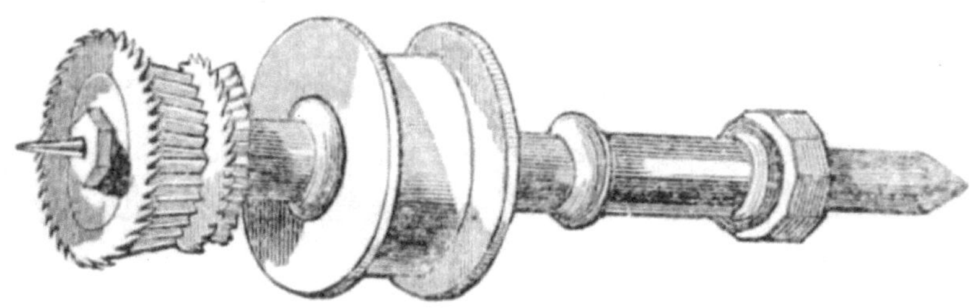

CUTTERS OF MR. PAXTON'S SASH-BAR MACHINE.

"There is one particular feature in working the machine, namely, the bar is presented to the saws below the centre of motion, instead of above it (as is usual); and to the sides of the saw which are ascending from the table, instead of those which are descending. These arrangements were necessary to suit the direction of the teeth to the grain of the wood; for when the bars were presented to the saws in the usual way, the wood was crushed instead of being cut and cleaned. It is essential that the machine should revolve 1,200 times in a minute to finish the work in a proper manner.

"The glass and glazing of the Chatsworth Conservatory caused me considerable thought and anxiety, as I was very desirous to do away altogether with the numerous overlaps connected with the old system of glazing with short lengths. This old method, even under the best of management, is certain, in the course of a few years, to render unsightly any structure, however well built.

"In the course of my inquiries, I heard that Messrs. Chance and Co., of Birmingham, had just introduced from the Continent the manufacture of sheet glass. Accordingly, I went to see them make this new article, and found they were able to manufacture it three feet in length. I was advised to use this glass in two lengths, with one overlap; but to this I could not assent, as I observed, that since they had so far advanced as to be able to produce sheets three feet in length, I saw no reason why they could not accomplish another foot; and, if this could not be done, I would decline giving the order, as, at that time, sheet glass was altogether an experiment for horticultural purposes. These gentlemen, however, shortly afterwards informed me that they had one person who could make it the desired length, and, if I would give the order, they would furnish me with all I required.

"It may just be remarked here that the glass for the Exhibition Building is forty-nine inches long—a size which no country except England is able to furnish in any large quantity, even at the present day.

"In 1840 the Chatsworth Conservatory was completed and planted. The whole length of this building is 277 feet; its breadth, 123 feet over the walls; and the height, from the floor to the highest part, 67 feet.

"Notwithstanding the success which attended the erection of these buildings, it became to me a question of importance how far an extensive structure might be covered in with *flat* ridge-and-furrow roofs; that is, the ridge-and-valley rafters placed on a level, instead of at an inclination, as in the green-house, or curvilinear, as in the Great Conservatory. I therefore prepared some plans for an erection of the kind for the Earl of Burlington, somewhere about ten years ago; but, on account of the lamented death of the Countess, the design of erection was abandoned. However, from that time I felt assured, not only that it could be done satisfactorily, but that the most appropriate manner to form and support level glass roofs, to a great extent, was that adopted this year for the New Victoria House at Chatsworth, which may be considered a miniature type of the Great Industrial Building.

"Before describing this house, however, it may be well to notice two instances in which the flat roofs had been previously tried, and in both cases with the most perfect success.

"The first of these was a conservatory attached to a villa in Darley Dale, only a short distance from Chatsworth. This building is divided into five bays, with a glass door in the centre, and glass pilasters separating the bays; the ridge-and-furrow roof covers an opening of seventeen feet in the clear. The ventilation is simultaneously effected by a lever connected with a rod, which is attached to all the ventilators....

THE VICTORIA REGIA HOUSE, CHATSWORTH.

"The second instance is this. In the spring of 1848, plans were prepared for the erection of an ornamental glass structure, to cover the conservatory wall at Chatsworth. This wall was previously a plain flued structure, devoted to the growth of rare and choice plants. The new erection is 331 feet in length, and 7 feet in width. It is divided into ten bays, with an ornamental centre projecting beyond the general line of the building. Each bay is subdivided by smaller bays, which are separated by glass pilasters; the glass sashes are so arranged that they can be removed in summer, and the whole thrown open to the gardens, whilst in winter the building affords an extensive promenade under cover. The ground on which this structure is built has a fall of 25 feet 6 inches in its whole length; consequently, there is a proportionate fall at each bay, which gives great variety, and obviates the monotony that would be exhibited in a building of such length and dimensions placed on a uniform level. The lower side of each bay is finished by a glass pilaster, three feet in width, and surmounted by a vase on the wall behind. The roof is on the ridge-and-furrow principle, with the rafters on a very slight inclination; and the ventilation is effected in a similar but more perfect manner than that already described as in use at the conservatory at Darley Dale.

"The new Victoria Regia House, which presents a light and novel appearance, is 60 feet 6 inches in length, and 46 feet 9 inches in breadth. Although, when compared with the Great Industrial Building, the Victoria House is a very diminutive structure, yet the principles on which it is constructed are the same, and may be carried out to an almost unlimited extent. The form of the roof, the general elevation, the supports, and the mode of construction, are all quite simple, and yet fully answer the purposes for which they were intended.

INTERIOR OF VICTORIA REGIA HOUSE.

"The Victoria House, however, was so built as to retain as much moisture and heat as possible, and yet to afford a strong and bright light at all seasons; whilst, on the contrary, the Industrial Building, being intended to accommodate a daily assemblage of many thousands of individuals, and a vast number of natural and mechanical productions, many of which would be destroyed by moisture and heat, is constructed so as fully to answer that end."

This, then, was the experience which enabled Mr. Paxton to conceive his design for the "Crystal Palace," a description of which as it has subsequently been carried out we must now proceed with.

GENERAL DESCRIPTION OF THE BUILDING

HE plan forms a parallelogram, 1,848 feet long and 408 feet wide, besides a projection on the north side, 48 feet wide and 936 feet long. A main avenue, 72 feet wide and 66 feet high, occupies the centre through the whole length of the building. Flanking this on either side are smaller avenues alternately 24 feet and 48 feet wide; the two first on either side of the centre are 43 feet, and the remainder 23 feet high. About the centre of the entire length, at a point determined by the position of a row of large trees, which it was resolved to inclose, these avenues are crossed by a transept of the same width as the main avenue, or 72 feet, and 108 feet high; two other groups of trees on the ground give occasion for open courts, which are inclosed within the building. The area thus inclosed and roofed over amounts to no less than 772,784 square feet, or about 19 acres;[4] the building is, therefore, about four times the size of St. Peter's at Rome, and more than six times that of St. Paul's, London. Three entrances lead to this vast interior, one in the centre of the principal or south front, and one at either end of the building. The number of these is necessarily small, in order to facilitate the arrangements for the money-taking, and to avoid having too large a staff of officers; on the other hand, it was equally desirable to afford the most ample opportunities of egress for visitors, and accordingly fifteen exit doors are placed at frequent intervals.

It will be well to mention here that the horizontal measure of 24 feet, which we have seen as the unit in the plan of the Building Committee, is also preserved in the present plan; every horizontal dimension of which is either a certain number of times or divisions of twenty-four feet.

---

[4] The surface covered by the Basilica of St. Peter's at Rome amounts to 223,900 square feet, the Cathedral at Milan occupies 124,100, and St. Paul's, London, 114,900 square feet.

GROUND-PLAN OF THE BUILDING.

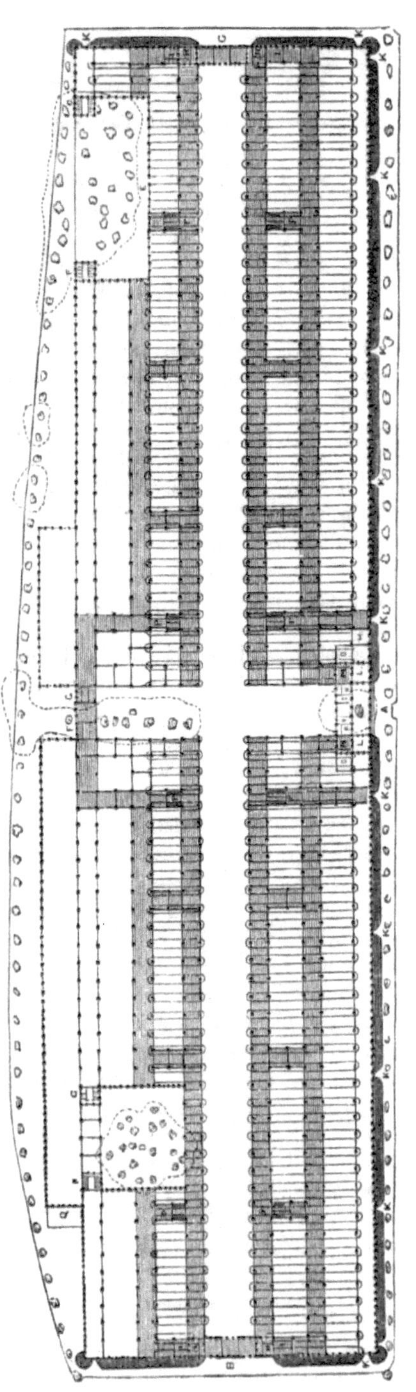

A. Principal Entrance.

B. West Entrance.

C. East Entrance.

D. Refreshment Courts.

E. Entrance.

F. Gentlemens' Ante-rooms.

G. Ladies' Ante-rooms.

H. Pay Place.

I. Accountant.

K. Exits.

L. Ante-rooms.

M. Committee Waiting-room.

N. Royal Commission.

O. Clerks.

P. Stairs.

Q. Engine House.

The avenues into which the plan is divided are formed by hollow cast-iron columns twenty-four feet apart, which rise in one, two, and three storeys respectively, to support the roof at the different heights given above; in the lower storey these columns are nineteen feet high, and in the two upper ones seventeen feet. Between the different lengths of the columns short pieces are introduced, called "connecting-pieces," from the office they perform; these are three feet long, and are so contrived that they serve to support girders in horizontal tiers, dividing the greatest height into three storeys as already mentioned. The girders, of which some are of cast and some of wrought iron, are all of the same depth, namely, three feet, with the exception of four, to be specially named hereafter, and by this arrangement the same horizontal lines are preserved throughout the whole of the building. They are also all similar in appearance, forming a kind of lattice-work, by which construction they do not look too heavy for the slight supports; and large solid masses are avoided, practically showing how great strength may be combined with elegance and lightness. The first or lower tier of these girders, in parts of the building more than one storey in height, forms the support for the floor of the galleries, which are twenty-four feet wide, and extend the whole length of the building in four parallel lines, intercepted only by the transept, round the ends of which they are continued. Numerous cross galleries connect each pair of longitudinal lines on either side of the centre avenue, which remains uninterrupted from end to end, and can only be crossed on the gallery-floor at the extremities.

These galleries are reached by eight double staircases, of easy ascent and ample width, which are placed between the lines of gallery so as to communicate equally readily with either, and are so distributed as to give two to each quarter of the building; in the eastern or foreign half two supplementary staircases of smaller dimensions have been added.

In those parts of the building more than two storeys in height, the second horizontal tier of girders does not support a gallery, but serves only to give stiffness to the columns. The upper tier of girders, in all cases, supports the roof, which is one of the most peculiar features in the structure. In its general form the roof is flat; but it is made up of a series of ridges and furrows, the rise and fall of which is but small, and is thus arranged: the roof-girders or trusses being twenty-four feet apart, and lying in the transverse direction of the building, the space between them is spanned by light beams or rafters, which are cambered or bent upwards, and are hollowed out in a groove on the top to form a gutter. The rafters are placed eight feet apart, their ends resting on the roof-girders, and lying, therefore, in the opposite direction to them, that is, in the direction of the length of the building; these rafters are commonly called the Paxton's Gutters. Between the rafters so described, *ridges* are supported by light sash-bars sloping up to them, at an inclination of two-and-a-half to one, and the rafter itself forms the bottom of the *furrow*. The advantage of this form of roofing is the facility it affords for the escape of the water, which runs from the surface of the roof into the Paxton's gutters; from them it is discharged into the main gutters resting on the roof-girders, by which it is conducted to the hollow columns, and passes down through them into the drains. A drop of water falling on the most distant point from the discharge would only have to traverse a distance of forty-eight feet; but in most cases the length to be passed over before reaching the down pipe would be considerably less.[5] The covering of the roof is glass, fixed between the sash-bars, which are grooved to receive it; and in order to carry off the moisture arising from condensation on the inner surface of the glass, the rafters have a small groove on each side, which makes the Paxton's gutter complete, and from which the moisture is also discharged into the main gutters. The essential portions of the roof may therefore be considered as a network of gutters; one set, the main gutters, lying in a transverse direction, and the others resting on them, and lying in the direction of the length of the building; by which arrangement any amount of surface can always be covered by roofing of a small span. The principle is precisely the same as that of subdividing large fields of arable land into strips or "lands" with furrows between them, in order to facilitate the surface-drainage.

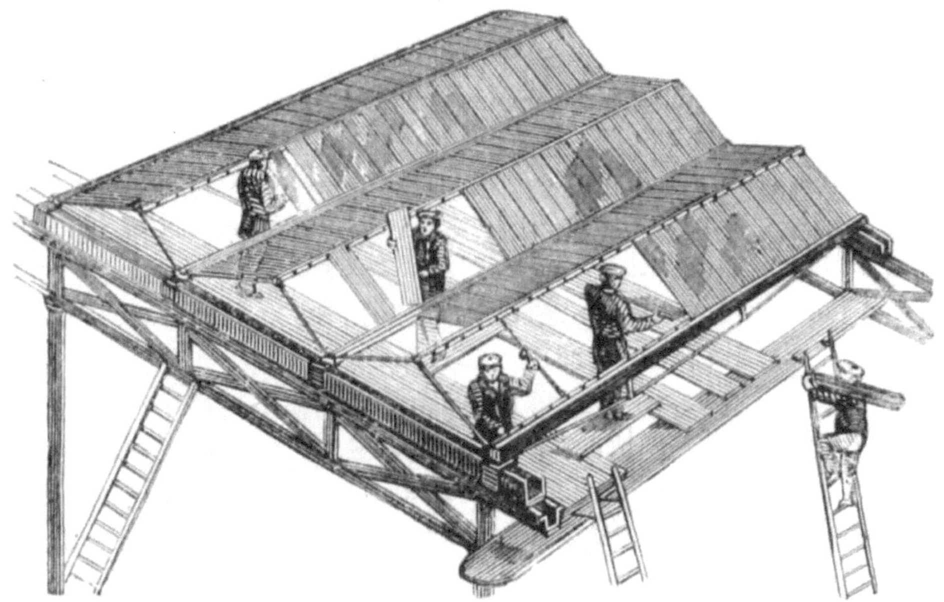

VIEW OF ONE 24-FEET SQUARE BAY OF ROOF PARTLY COMPLETED.

The outer inclosure, on the ground-floor, is formed by dividing each 24-feet bay between the columns into three 8-feet bays by half columns of wood, between which is placed boarding, held in its place by iron clips and bolts; a plinth, four feet high, is formed immediately above the floor by frames, filled with what are commonly called louvre-blades, which are hung on pivots, and of which a large number can be moved simultaneously for the admission of air; similar ventilating-frames, three feet deep, are introduced at the top of each storey round the entire circuit of the building, and by this means a ventilating-surface of no less than

[5] It is perhaps necessary to mention here, that the leakage of the roof which was at first much complained of was owing to incomplete construction, and not to any defect in the principle, or in the manner in which it has been carried out.

40,800 square feet is obtained, or rather more than one acre.

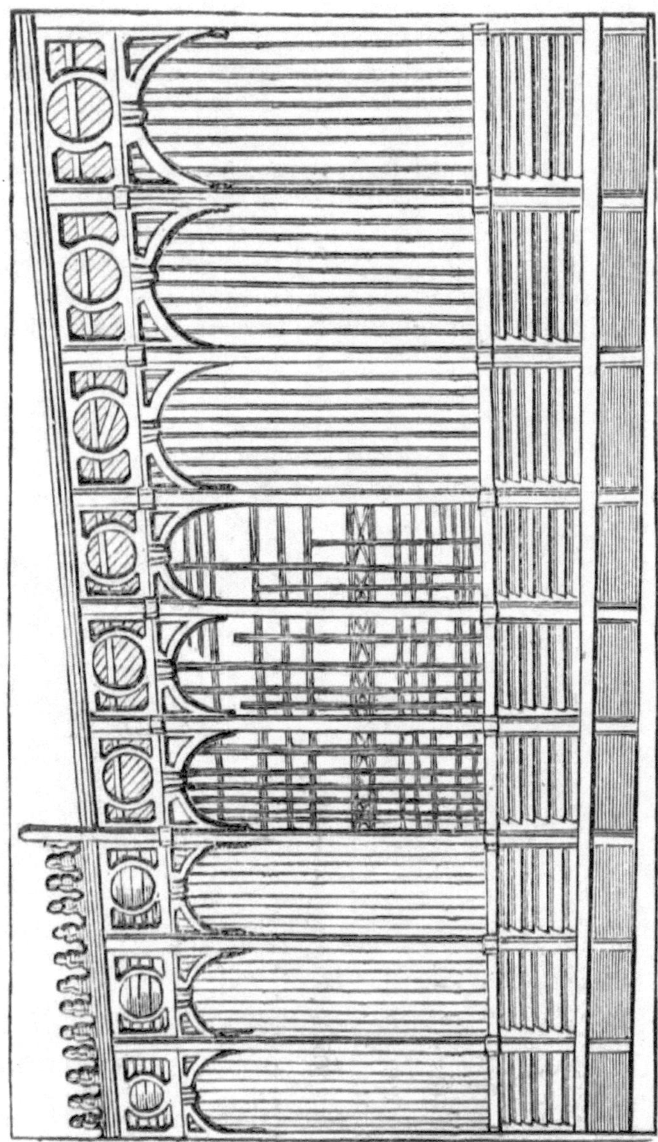

PORTION OF THE LOWER STOREY OF THE PRINCIPAL ELEVATIONS.

Externally some light arches are inserted, and open panels form the inclosure for the upper louvre-frames. The details we have been describing may be readily traced in the engraving of a portion of the lower storey as seen from the outside. The exit doors occupy one of the 8-feet bays opening about six feet wide. The inclosure to the upper storeys closely resembles those of the ground-floor, but glazed sashes are substituted for the close boarding, and the plinth is omitted. Each storey is crowned externally with a cornice and cresting ornament, and over the columns posts are carried up, to which flagstaffs will be fixed.

To return to the interior. The whole of the floor is boarded; that below is laid with an interval of half an inch between the boards, to allow the passage of dust from the millions of feet by which it will be trod; the gallery floor, on the contrary, has iron tongues between the boards to prevent the dust from coming through on the heads of the visitors below.

The roof of the transept, which we have described as crossing the building about the centre of its length, differs from that of the other parts, its general form being semicircular instead of flat, and rising above the rest of the building so as to show the whole of the semicircle externally. This roof is supported by arched timber ribs placed twenty-four feet apart, or one over every column, which forms a socket, into which the foot of the rib is fitted and secured by iron straps. Between the ribs, timbers are fixed which carry minor ribs at a distance of eight feet apart, and upon these the ridge-and-furrow roofing is constructed in the manner that has been described for the flat roofing, but following the curve of the arched ribs. At the springing or foot of the arch on either side of the transept there is a range of louvre-frames to assist in the ventilation of the building, and on the top of the arch externally a narrow passage is formed to give access to the different parts of this roof. On the inner side of the arch diagonal tie-rods are introduced between the main ribs, which, while they serve to increase the strength of the construction by tying together all the parts from end to end, produce an agreeable play of lines forming a kind of network over the whole of the surface.

The ends of the transept are closed in with fan-like tracery, reminding the spectator of the magnificent wheel windows of our Gothic cathedrals; this elegant feature is not visible in our interior view, but will be seen in some of the exteriors.

There is, perhaps, no part of this interesting building in which the great size and singular lightness, almost airiness, of the construction are so strikingly displayed as in the TRANSEPT, inclosing as it does a row of fine old elm-trees, as if to protect them in their venerable age from the smoke of the thousands of chimneys that have been gradually forming a destructive circle around them.

The only portion of solid untransparent roofing in the whole of this building is formed on either side of the arched roof just described, where there is a lead flat twenty-four feet wide. This was partly required for a platform to serve for carrying on the works for the arched roof, and was also exceedingly useful in giving access to the other roofs on either side; it likewise afforded the opportunity of giving some additional strength at the springing of the arched ribs to resist any possible tendency they might have to spread outwards.

VIEW OF THE INTERIOR OF THE TRANSEPT.

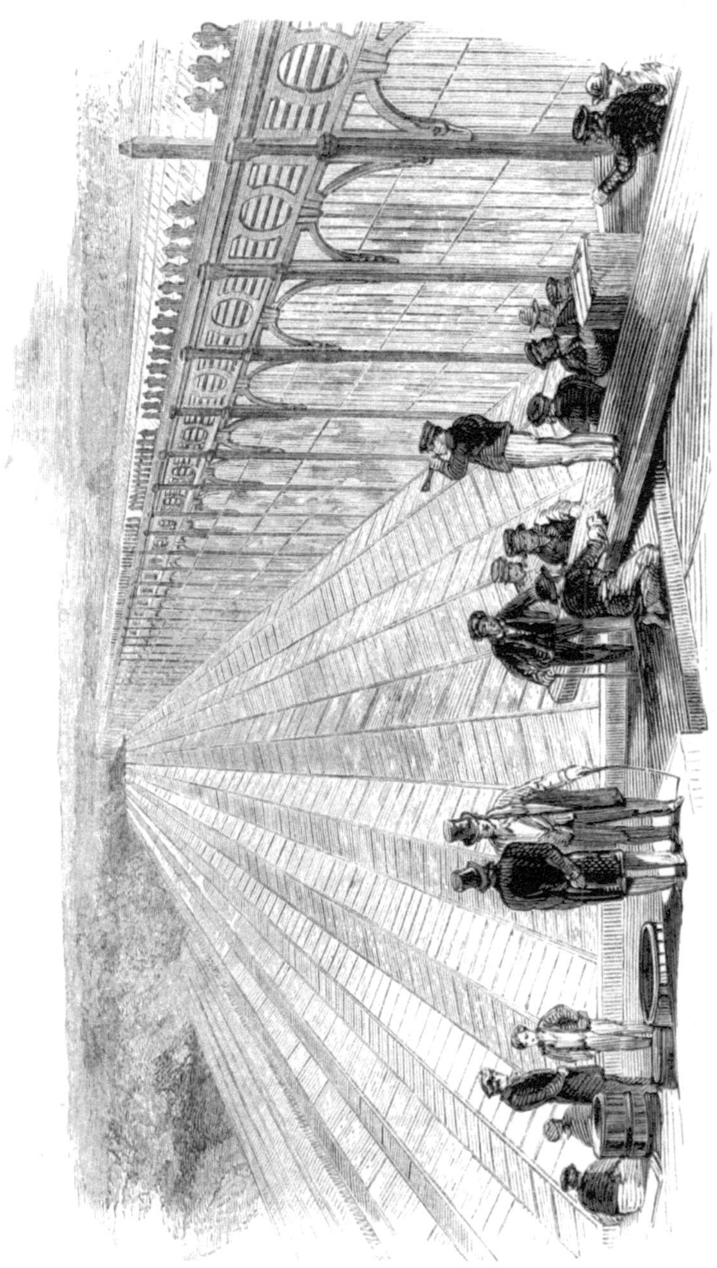

VIEW OF GLASS ROOF FROM THE LEAD FLAT.

As the weight of such lead roofing considerably exceeds that of the glass ridge-and-furrow covering, it was necessary at the point where it crosses the wide span of the main avenue to introduce some stronger roof-girders than those used elsewhere; of these there are two on either side of the transept, the inner one of which has also to sustain two of the large arched ribs with their superincumbent roofing, and its strength is therefore increased in proportion to the additional load placed upon it. The extra-strong roof-girders are six feet deep, or twice that of the others; but their general construction is similar, the diagonal ties forming a kind of latticework, and thus keeping up the same character. These, like all the roof-girders of large span, are constructed principally of wrought-iron. Those who visited the building during its erection, and were among the fortunate few who were enabled to ascend to the "lead-flat," must have been very much struck with the singular appearance presented by the great expanse of acres of glass stretching in long lines of "ridge-and-furrow" roofing on each side of the centre, while the eye, penetrating the transparent covering, became lost in endeavouring to follow the apparently intricate lines of the interior. Such a view might fairly be said to justify the title of "Crystal Palace," by which this building is so commonly known; and it would require no great stretch of imagination to believe that it had been reared by fairy hands, as a votive offering at the world's jubilee of labour.

But we must descend again to the interior, to point out the arrangement of the offices for the staff of the Executive. The principal of these are naturally placed in the centre, on either side of the principal entrance, where they occupy in two storeys the space underneath the gallery, which is continued uninterrupted over them. The entrances at the end are also flanked by offices of less extent. The outer inclosure of these spaces is formed with glazed sashes, similar to those which are placed on the exterior of the building, and boarded partitions divide the interior. The rooms are arranged to be heated and lighted by gas when required, and ample means of ventilation are provided.

The simplicity of the construction renders it very easy to extend or contract the accommodation much more readily than would be possible under ordinary circumstances.

It now remains to notice the arrangements provided for refreshments, which are introduced in connexion with the open courts left on account of the groups of trees. These happen to occur towards the ends of the building, and on the north side of the main avenue; the space at the north end of the transept, next to the inclosed trees, is also appropriated for this purpose. The roofing over these parts is a continuation of that over the rest of the building; and the partitions necessary for inclosing the different spaces are formed chiefly with glazed sashes, avoiding as much as possible any solid construction, which would appear out of character. The open courts are inclosed with sashes and doors, rendered necessary by the uncertain nature of our climate.

A small detached building which has not been mentioned serves for the boiler-house, and is placed near the west end of the building. As it had been determined to afford the means of exhibiting some of the machinery in actual motion, it was necessary to erect boilers to supply the steam to the different machines, as it would clearly be inadmissible for each to generate steam for its own use in the building. The house to contain the boilers is ninety-six feet long and twenty-four feet wide, and is placed as near as practicable to the machinery-department; but at the same time it is quite detached from the main building to avoid risk from the fires. In appearance it resembles the one-storey portion of the main building, but it is constructed entirely of fire-proof materials. It contains five boilers, each to supply steam for twenty-horse power, which is distributed by a pipe to the different machinery.

GENERAL VIEW OF THE BUILDING FROM THE SOUTH-WEST.

An ornamental cast-iron railing designed by Mr. Owen Jones incloses the building, being placed at a distance of about eight feet from it along the principal fronts, but carried much further off at the ends, so as to inclose a considerable space, which will thus be available for exhibiting any large objects that will bear exposure to the weather, if there should not be sufficient room in the interior of the building. Gates are placed opposite all the entrances and exits, and these are so arranged that when closed they are uniform in appearance with the rest of the railing.

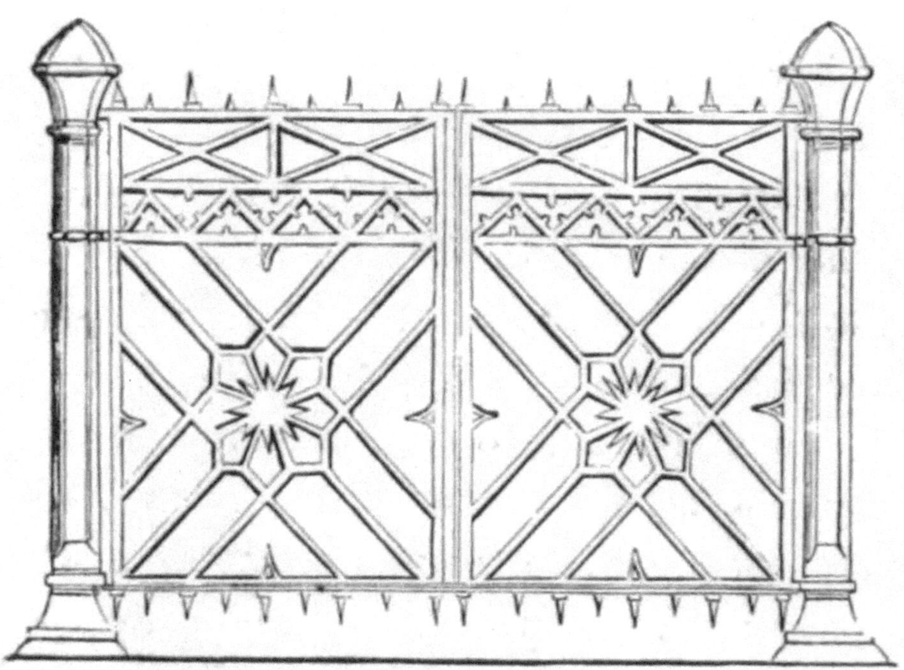

EXTERNAL RAILING.

Having thus given a general sketch of the arrangement and appearance of the building, we shall proceed to describe somewhat more minutely the various details of the construction, of which the essential parts are few in number compared with the great repetition of each individually. To assist in this multiplied reproduction of the same form, some exceedingly ingenious machinery has been employed, which will therefore be described in connexion with the parts it has been used to form; and thus these will be traced through their various stages, from the raw material to their finished state as portions of the building. The greater part of this machinery has been used in shaping out those parts which are of wood, and particularly the different portions of the roof, with which we will therefore commence.

THE PAXTON'S GUTTERS

T has been mentioned that the rafters which span the space between the roof-girders serve, at the same time, as gutters, for which purpose they are hollowed out on the upper face, besides having smaller grooves at the sides to take the condensation-water. The bottom of the gutter is of a circular form, which is universally considered the best for conveying liquids with the least amount of friction, and therefore the least liable to obstruction from an accumulation of dirt.

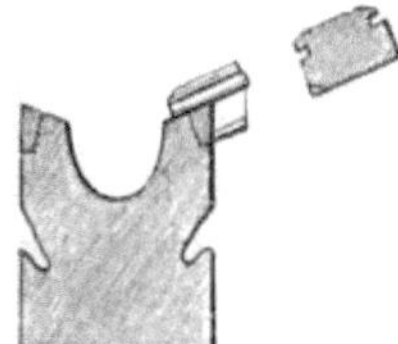

SECTION OF THE PAXTON'S GUTTER, WITH THE STRONG SASH-BAR.

THE CIRCULAR PLANING-MACHINE.

PORTION OF PLANING-MACHINE, WITH THE REVOLVING ARM AND CUTTERS.

A section of the gutter, as finished, is shown. To bring it into this form, after the timbers had been sawn into the requisite general dimensions they were brought under the action of the planing-machine, where they were planed on the four sides. This machine is patented by W. Furness, of Liverpool, and was worked at the Chelsea Wharf Saw-mills. The operation was effected by cutters (*a*) attached to the ends of an arm revolving with great rapidity in a horizontal plane; the timbers to be planed were wedged up into a frame (*b*) traversing on rails, and as this was passed under the revolving cutters the upper surface was removed by them, at the same time the timbers were held down upon the frame by a large iron disc (*c*) pressing upon their upper surface. The disc, together with the revolving arm carrying the cutters, was capable of being adjusted vertically to the exact dimensions of the timber. The traversing-frame was slowly propelled by the machinery, and three widths of timber were operated upon at one time. On leaving the planing-machine these quarter baulks were passed on to the gutter-cutting machine. Four different cutters were required to form the section, as shown above; they were placed one behind the other, so that the piece of timber, which was presented to their action above the centre of motion, passed over each of them in succession. The first set, which revolved in a vertical plane, roughly hollowed out the larger groove to the section shown in Fig. 1; the two next were counterparts, and formed the same section in opposite directions; they were set at an inclination to the upright of about 45 degrees, the one to the right, the other to the left; and each hollowed out one of the small side grooves, and one side of the larger gutter, leaving the section of the timber respectively of the forms shown in Figs. 2 and 3. Fig. 4 shows the form of its section after it had passed both; the fourth set of cutters again revolved vertically, and gave the gutter its finished form, as shown above. As the timber passed over the cutters it was supported at the ends on revolving rollers, and was held in its place by guiding grooves, being pressed gradually forwards against the cutters.

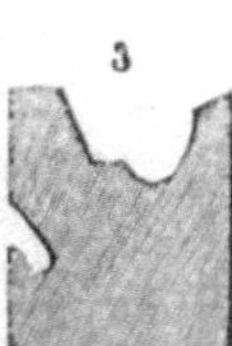
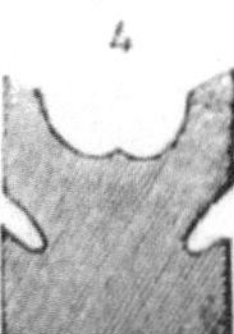

SECTIONS OF THE DIFFERENT STAGES OF THE PAXTON'S GUTTERS.

THE GUTTER-CUTTING MACHINE.

In this manner forty-two lengths of solid gutter, each twenty-four feet and a fraction long, were completed in a day of ten hours; and as the machine was worked double time, a length of more than 2,000 feet was turned out daily ready for use: this, it has been calculated, would have required the labour of about three hundred men to be employed for the same length of time. The absolute necessity for such rapid production will be evident when it is known that no less than 110,000 feet, or about twenty miles length, of such gutters were required—very nearly the distance from Buckingham Palace to Windsor Castle.

Finished as described above, the Paxton's gutters arrived at the building, where the first operation they underwent was that of cutting them to the exact length requisite. This was a nice operation, as the smallest deviation would have caused a difficulty in fitting them into their place, and to perform it a framework was constructed by which the solid gutter could be bent to the same curve it would have when fixed; a precaution that was necessary in order that the ends might be cut off quite vertically so as to fit together when in their place. At one end of this frame-work was placed a circular saw, twenty inches diameter, hung with a pulley and balance weight, so as to be moved up and down by means of a lever. The gutter being fixed in the frame by means of hinged guage-plates, one end was cut by the circular saw being brought down upon it; and at the same time another operation was performed: two cutters, placed in the centre of the circular saw, were so arranged that when brought down upon the end of the solid gutter they cut out a semi-circular notch, so that when the ends of two gutters were afterwards placed together there was a circular hole left, through which the water passed down into the main gutter. When these operations were completed at one end of the gutter, the guage-plates were taken off, and the timber was swung round on a pivot or crutch in the centre, and the same process gone through as before; the whole scarcely occupying two minutes. We shall presently have to return to this piece of machinery, as it was also used in finishing the ridge rafters.

MACHINE FOR FINISHING ENDS OF GUTTERS AND RIDGES.

The solid gutter was now transferred to the hands of the carpenter, who fixed at each end, on the under-side, a small cast-iron shoe; and two struts, nine inches long, were placed so as to divide the whole length into three equal parts—the struts spread out at the top in order to present a large surface of pressure against the under-side of the gutter; and tenons projected upwards, which were fitted into mortices cut into the timber. The lower end of the struts were formed so as to give them a firm hold upon a wrought-iron rod, thirteen-sixteenths of an inch diameter, which was passed under them and through the shoes, where it was screwed up with nuts; and the struts pressing up against the timber produced the requisite bend or camber. Twenty-seven notches, to receive the sash bars, were marked with a templet and cut out on each edge of the upper-side of the gutter; and a small cast-iron plate having been fitted on the under-side at each end, the Paxton's gutter was complete and ready for fixing. The under-trussing of the rafters increased their strength considerably, so that a weight of one-and-a-half tons was required to break one which was experimented upon.

THE SASH-BARS

E will next consider the sash-bars which support the ridge of the roof and receive the glass. The total length which was required of these amounts to about two hundred miles; it will, therefore, be easily understood that mechanical contrivance for cutting them out became an absolute necessity; this Mr. Paxton appears to have discovered in his works at Chatsworth, as he mentions in his lecture.

MACHINE FOR CUTTING OUT SASH-BARS.

The sash-bars are one inch thick and one-and-a-half inches deep, and are grooved on each side, besides having all the four edges bevelled or chamfered; all which was done in one passage through the machine. The plank which was to form the sash-bars was passed in at one end of the machine, between pressure-rollers; it then passed between cutters placed both above and below it, which made about twelve hundred revolutions per minute, and hollowed out the different grooves; and, lastly, it passed between circular saws which divided it into separate sash-bars, after which they had only to be cut into their proper lengths.[6]

[6] About three hundred planks were passed through the machine in a working-day of ten hours, allowing the necessary stoppages for sharpening the cutters; and if only three widths of sash-bar were produced out of each blank, the quantity finished per diem would

The exact length of each sash-bar when finished is four feet one inch.

In this state the skylight bars were sent to the building, where they underwent several finishing operations, necessary to make the ends fit down into the notches prepared in the ridges and gutters. Thirty of the bars were first placed together in a horizontal traversing-frame on a saw-table, on each side of which circular saws were fixed at the distance of the required length of the sash-bar; the frame was then moved forward against the saws, so that both ends of the whole set of bars were cut off simultaneously, and at the same time a cut was made at one end half-way through the bar, in order to form the shoulder against the gutter. They were then removed to another bench, where the end of the bar was bevelled and the shoulder formed by means of a small instrument having a handle with two projecting jaws fitting into the ends of the glass grooves of the bars; between these there was a small blade which, being pressed down, cut out the shoulder which had been sawn through in the other direction, and another blade was placed at the proper angle to remove the bevelled piece at the end of the bar.

THE SASH-BAR DRILLING-MACHINE.

One more process made the sash-bars complete for fixing—this was the drilling a hole at each end to nail them down on the gutter and ridge; and this was also done by machinery, to insure all the holes being drilled at the same angle. On one side of a horizontal bench were placed a set of four-inch driving pulleys (*a a*), with as many horizontal drills projecting towards the other side of the bench; a wooden traversing-plate (*c*) opposite each drill, and working towards it, received one end amount to about two miles and three quarters. This machinery, as well as that for grooving and moulding the ridges, was worked at the Phoenix Saw-mills, Cumberland-basin, Regent's Park, belonging to Mr. Birch.

of the sash-bar, while the other rested in an inclined position against a wooden rail (*b*) placed longitudinally above the pulleys, having as many sinkings thereon as there were drills. The traversing-plate being then pushed forward, the sash-bar was perforated by the drill; the plate was then drawn back, and the same operation repeated with the other end of the bar, which left it ready for fixing.

The action of the traversing-plate (*c*) is shown more distinctly in the second engraving.[7] One out of every nine of the sash-bars of the roof is stronger than the rest, to serve for fixing the ridge previous to glazing. These extra-strong bars are two inches wide and one inch and a half deep, and were formed by the same machinery already described, by an adjustment of the different cutters and saws.

PORTION OF SASH-BAR DRILLING-MACHINE.

---

[7] A This piece of machinery is only novel in its application, as it is similar to that used by brush-makers for drilling a number of small holes in close and regular arrangement.

THE RIDGES

HE total length of these required was about sixteen miles. They are cut out of timber three inches square, in section, and are of the form shown in the diagram, with a groove on each side to receive the glass. This was also done by machinery which, with about five-horse power, turned out one hundred lengths of twenty-four feet in a day of ten hours, allowing the time for the necessary stoppages. After they had been delivered at the building, these ridge-pieces were cut to the exact lengths by means of the same apparatus used for the solid gutters which has already been described. At each end of the ridge-piece two holes were also drilled to receive dowells to connect it with the adjoining length. By no other than mechanical means could the immense number of holes thus drilled have been placed so exactly that those in the opposite ends of any two ridge-pieces should correspond precisely.

SECTION OF RIDGE AND ORDINARY SASH-BAR.

The different essential component parts of the roof having thus been described, we propose to take the different members of the construction in succession downwards.

THE GLASS

UT first it may be mentioned here that the glass used throughout the building is sheet, on an average about one-sixteenth of an inch thick, and weighing one pound per foot superficial. This gives an aggregate weight of about four hundred tons for the whole of the work, the greater part of which was supplied by Messrs. Chance and Co., of Birmingham. Each square is forty-nine inches long and ten wide, the greatest length of sheet glass that has ever been made in this country. The manufacture of this kind of glass is of comparatively recent introduction into England, though practised for some time on the Continent; and the rapid progress made by the manufacturers alluded to must be in a great measure attributed to the wise removal of the fiscal burden on the article, made by the late Sir Robert Peel. That lamented statesman, with his usual foresight, doubtless contemplated that great social benefits would follow from that enactment; and it is, perhaps, not too much to say that, but for Sir Robert's enlightened measure, this "huge pile of transparency" would never have been reared.

THE BOX GUTTERS

T has been mentioned that the triple gutters deliver the water into main gutters running in the transverse direction of the building; these are formed of wood, with a bottom piece, into which are grooved two upright sides, they are firmly bolted down upon the upper flange of the roof-girders, and where these are quite horizontal the fall in the gutter is given by a false bottom laid to a slope. Of these gutters there is a length of about five-and-a-half miles in the building, which, added to the aggregate length of the Paxton's gutters, makes a total of about twenty-five-and-a-half miles of gutter.

THE ROOF GIRDERS

HESE are of cast-iron, where not more than twenty-four feet long, and the rest of wrought-iron. The cast-iron ones are precisely the same in appearance as those used for the galleries, but lighter in metal; a separate description of them is not, therefore, necessary. The weight of each of these girders is twelve cwt., and each was proved to nine tons previously to being used; but it is calculated that the greatest weight they may have to bear will not exceed five tons: the total number required was about 470.

The wrought-iron girders, or trusses, are partly forty-eight and partly seventy-two feet long, to span the avenues of those respective widths; the principle of the construction is the same in each. The top rail (if it may be so called) of the truss is formed with two pieces of **L** iron placed back to back , **⌐Γ** and the bottom rail with two flat bars **І І**, the total depth being three feet; at the ends these bars are riveted on to cast-iron standards, and the intermediate distance is divided into eight-feet lengths by other cast-iron standards, to which the bars are also riveted, and thus a framework of rectangles is formed. In the trusses forty-eight feet span there are, therefore, six such divisions in the length, and nine in those of seventy-two feet span. These are then divided in the direction of ONE of the diagonals by a flat bar passing between and riveted to those forming the top and bottom rails. This completes the constructional part of the truss; but to render the appearance more uniform with that of the cast-iron girders, a flat bar of wood (shown by the dotted lines) is made to form the other diagonal of the rectangles.

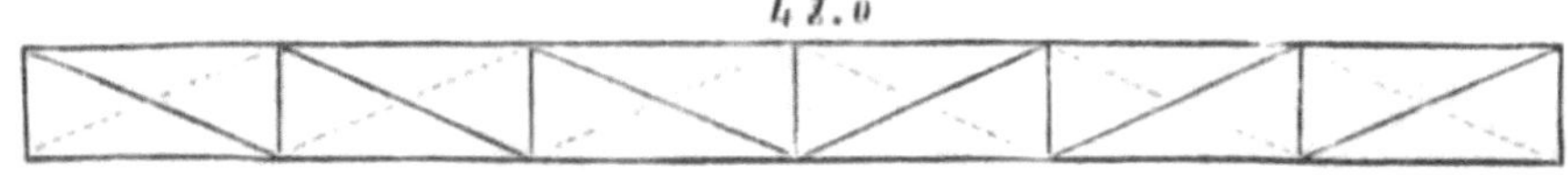

DIAGRAM OF 48-FEET GIRDER.

The trusses for a span of seventy-two feet are cambered or bent upwards about ten inches, which both adds to their strength and improves the appearance. The form and arrangement of these roof-trusses may be clearly traced in several of the views of the interior which are presented to the reader. The weight, when completed, of each of the trusses of seventy-two feet span is about thirty-five cwt., and of those of forty-eight feet span about thirteen cwt.

It has been already mentioned that four of the roof-trusses vary from the rest on account of the greater load they have to sustain. The depth of these exceptional trusses is six feet, and their length seventy-two feet, or the width of the main avenue, which they bridge over. The principle of their construction is similar to that employed in the lighter trusses; but the arrangement of the parts is somewhat modified. The top rail consists of two pieces of **L** iron, placed, as before, back to back; but they are further connected on the top by a flat piece **⊤⊤**. The lower rail is formed by two flat bars placed upright **| |**, and these are riveted at the ends to standards of cast-iron, which, however, are considerably heavier in construction than those before described; and they have also in the centre, at (*a*) two slots, or sinkings, into which the ends of two of the diagonal bars are riveted. The whole length is then divided into three equal parts, each 24 feet long, by strong CAST-iron standards at (*b*) the ends of which are riveted between the rails, and these spaces are again subdivided into three eight-feet lengths by WROUGHT-iron standards at (*c c*). The top of each standard is next connected with the foot of the next but one to it by diagonal flat bars, which, together with the short pieces fastened into the slots at (*a*), complete the figure of the whole, forming a kind of trellis-work, two diamonds in depth. In the diagram only half the length of the girder is shown.

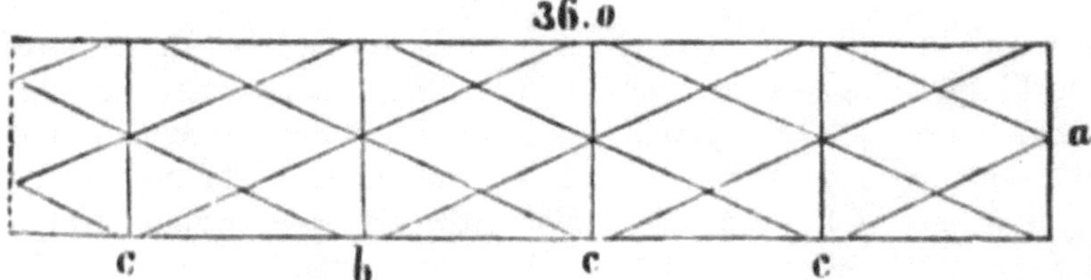

DIAGRAM OF ONE-HALF OF 72-FEET GIRDER.

The dimensions of the different bars of iron in this piece of construction are proportional to the amount of strain they have to bear. The two heavier out of the four trusses just described weighed when completed eight tons each, and the other two, which are of rather lighter construction, six tons each.

The riveting together of the wrought-iron trusses was performed on horizontal supports, on which the curve that they were to be made to was marked out. The bars having been previously cut to the requisite lengths, and punched and drilled with holes for the rivets, were laid out on the stages in the proper forms with the cast-iron standards, which were temporarily kept in place by bolts passed through some of the rivet-holes. The whole framework was then riveted up with red-hot rivets supplied from small portable furnaces, several sets of men being employed upon each truss, by which means as many as sixteen were completed in one day. The whole of the trusses, three hundred and seventy-two in number, required for the building were put together on the ground, and several ingenious mechanical contrivances were made use of to facilitate and hasten the work. To form some idea of the amount of labour that had to be performed, it may be mentioned that each of the trusses forty-eight feet in length, or the smallest, is held together by more than fifty rivets, requiring more than twice that number of holes to be made in bars of iron varying in thickness from a quarter of an inch upwards. About 25,000 rivets were thus required for the whole of the work.

THE IRON DRILLING MACHINE

HE holes for the rivets were made partly by drilling and partly by punching. In the machine used for the former the bar to be bored was laid upon a flat surface forming part of the solid cast-iron stand of the machinery; the drilling-point worked vertically, and could be moved in that direction to suit the different thicknesses of iron brought under its operation. It was suspended at one end of a lever, with a counterpoise at the other. This lever was also connected by a rod and crank, with another near the ground, one end of which was formed into a tread to be worked by the foot. The workman, when he had arranged the iron in the right position under the drill, pressed his foot upon the tread; thus raising the counterpoise end of the upper lever, and pressing the point of the drill, which was of a spear-head form, down upon the iron. Underneath the iron to be drilled was placed a piece of wood to protect the point of the drill when it had passed through the iron. It was also necessary to moisten the iron during the operation, in order to keep the drill-point cool. Three men were required to attend to this work, which was not so rapid as the other method of making the holes by punching.

THE DRILLING-MACHINE.

THE PUNCHING MACHINE

THE PUNCHING-MACHINE AND SHEARS.

HE enormous power exerted by this piece of machinery renders it necessary that the stand containing the punch, &c., should be exceedingly solid, and it is formed accordingly by a heavy mass of cast-iron, in which there are two indentations, as seen by the engraving. In the lower of these the punching operation is performed, and in the upper there are shears for cutting off the ends of the bars when required. The motion is communicated to each of these by means of a cogged wheel at the back; but both the punch and the shears work in a vertical direction, slowly moving up and down with irresistible force. There is no sudden blow or jerk, which makes the effect the more striking, as the unpractised eye has no means of discovering the amount of the force which is being put in operation. It is, however, so great that, although the punching of a hole scarcely occupies two or three seconds, the iron becomes quite hot from the effect of the pressure. In using this machine, the workman arranges the iron bar on a solid rest, placing it so that when the punch descends it makes the hole in the position required. As soon as the punch has passed through the bar, the action of the machinery is reversed, and the instrument ascends again; during which time the bar is re-arranged, and the operation is thus continually repeated. This piece of machinery also requires three men to work it, if the bars to be punched are of considerable length, so as to require the ends to be held up; otherwise, one alone is sufficient; and in the course of a ten-hours day about three thousand holes can be punched out—the number, of course, varying according to the thickness of the bars.

Neither of the mechanical contrivances just described are novel inventions, though they are thus, perhaps, brought for the first time under the notice of many of our readers, to whom they may be so far rendered interesting from their being connected with the execution of THE building of the day.

THE ADZING AND PLANING MACHINE

THE ADZING-CUTTERS.

T the Chelsea Saw-mills, where the reader has already seen the Paxton's gutters shaped out, another interesting piece of machinery was in use for these works, for the purpose of finishing planks to a certain size and thickness, called the adzing and planing machine. An adze is a tool used by carpenters to remove any unevenness in the surface of a board in a particular spot. In this piece of machinery two cutters are fixed to a revolving arm, under which the plank is made to pass; and as it does so the cutters remove a certain thickness from the whole of the surface. The arrangement of these cutters is very plainly shown in the annexed engraving. On the under-side of the same bench to which this apparatus is fixed, three planes are set, each at an angle of about 5 degrees, by which the under-side of the plank is brought to an even face, while the upper surface is operated on by the adzing-cutters, and in this manner the plank is reduced to an even thickness throughout. As it passes on it is brought between two circular saws, which are adjusted to the width which it is desired to give to the plank. It is dragged forward towards the planes and cutters by means of an endless chain, composed of open links; which chain passes over a wheel provided with projecting pegs, so arranged as to fit into the links. The plank is kept down upon the planes, and otherwise held in position, by pressure-rollers.

THE ADZING AND PLANING MACHINE.

THE COLUMNS AND CONNECTING-PIECES

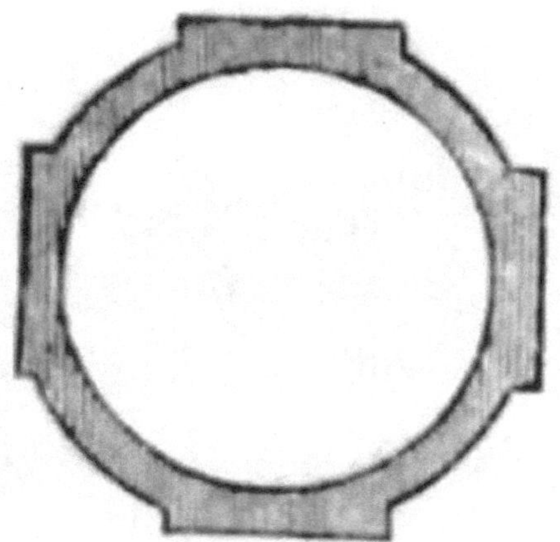

SECTION OF COLUMN.

HE columns in the building perform three important offices. They support the roof and the galleries, and serve as pipes to convey the rain-water from the roofs. Their form, which is beautiful, both mechanically and artistically, was suggested by Mr. Barry; it is a ring, eight inches in diameter externally, the thickness varying in the different columns, according to the weights they have to support respectively. Four flat faces, about three inches wide, are added on the outside of this ring, so that when the column is in its place, they face nearly north, south, east, and west. The column may therefore be considered as a hollow tube, of the section just described, and of the same form at each end, having at its extremities horizontally projecting rings called SNUGS, through which the bolts are passed, to fasten the columns to the connecting-pieces and base-pieces. That the hollow form adopted for the columns is that best suited to obtain the greatest strength with the least amount of material has been abundantly shown by experiments, as even two straws placed in an upright position will bear a very considerable weight; it is that also seen in the structure of the bones of animals. Of these columns there are 3,300 in the whole building.

Those portions of the height of the columns which correspond with the depth and position of the girders form separate lengths, which are called connecting-pieces, as they unite the lengths of columns of the different storeys. These connecting-pieces have the same sectional form as the columns themselves, and, like them, are the same at each end, where there are projections cast on, which serve to support the girders, and which are provided with holes through which the bolts pass to connect them with the columns. These holes alternate with the projections to receive the girders, which projections are so formed that they clip others cast on to the ends of the girders, which will be hereafter described. In the centre of each projection there is formed a small notch which receives the key or wedge for fixing the girders.

The meeting faces of the columns and connecting-pieces were all turned in a lathe, in order that, when set up, they might fit so precisely as not to require any packing to adjust them in an upright position; and only in the cases of those columns which serve as water-pipes is any such packing introduced. In those a piece of canvass, with white lead, is put into the joint. An enormous amount of additional labour was involved by this proceeding, as no less than twelve hundred of such faces had to be operated on; but this did not deter the enterprising contractors, who were fully alive to the importance of the object to be attained. When fixed, the projecting "snugs," with the bolts passing through them, were covered by ornamental caps and bases of cast-iron, fixed after the rest of the work was completed.

THE BASE-PIECES

HE lower storey of columns in every case stands upon base-pieces of which the upright portion is a continuation of the column, with "snugs" at the top, to correspond with those of the column, and standing on a horizontal bed-plate, from which "shoulders" rise to strengthen the upright portion. These bed-plates vary in size from three feet by two feet to one foot six inches by one foot, in proportion to the weight which the several superincumbent columns have to sustain. The longest dimension of the bed-plate is in the transverse direction of the building, in which the greatest overturning strain might be expected to act upon the columns. From the vertical portion of the base-pieces, sockets six inches in diameter project, in the direction of the length of the building, into which are fitted the cast-iron drain-pipes, which convey away the water brought down by the columns from the roof. The height of the base-pieces varies to suit the different levels at which the floor is supported above the ground. These levels had therefore to be determined in every individual instance previous to the castings being made. It was done, however, with such precision that, when they came to be used, they were all found to be of the exact length required for their situation. Of these base-pieces, 1,074 were required for the building.

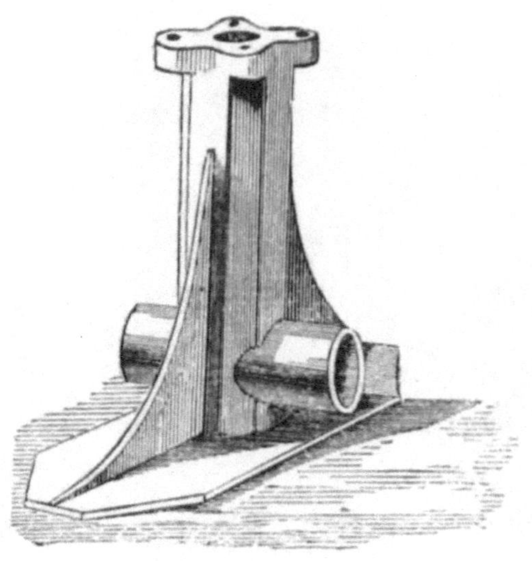

BASE-PIECE.

THE CAST-IRON GIRDERS

T has been mentioned that the columns supported girders at three different heights, dividing the greatest altitude of the building into three storeys; and that the lower tier of girders, where the building consisted of more than one storey, served to support a gallery.

These gallery girders are all twenty-four feet long and three feet deep, the upper and lower "flanges" or rails having a **T** formed section with standards at the ends of similar section. The rectangular space between them is then divided into three equal parts, by uprights having a **+** form of section, and the three smaller spaces thus obtained have diagonal "struts" in each direction. The girder thus described forms a double truss, in which the diagonal braces are subjected both to the strain of compression and tension. At the top and bottom of the end-standards small projections are cast on, by which the connecting-pieces hold the girders; and at each end of the flat portion of the top and bottom rails small sinkings are cast, by means of which the girder is keyed up to its position. The flat portion of the upper and lower "flanges" of the girder is swelled out in width from the ends towards the centre, in order to increase the quantity of metal in that part where the strain is greatest.

The description just given of the gallery girders will apply to all the cast-iron girders throughout the building, of which there are 2,150; the only difference between them being, that those for the roofs or other internal portions, where no gallery is to be supported, are cast with a less amount of metal. The form of girder just described, which is unusual, was the result of several experiments performed under the superintendence of Messrs. W. Cubitt, C. H. Wild, C. Fox, and other gentlemen, previous to the commencement of the building; and the thickness of metal for the different parts of these, as well as for all the other cast-iron work in the building, was minutely calculated and determined by Mr. C. H. Wild and Mr. C. Fox, under the supervision of Mr. Cubitt, the President of the Institution of Civil Engineers, to whom the Royal Commission had intrusted the responsible duty of the chief superintendence of the whole of the work.

VIEW OF INTERIOR FROM THE LEVEL OF GALLERIES.

THE GALLERIES

O proceed to the gallery itself, supported by the girders just described. The timbers supporting the floor are so arranged that the weight of each bay of twenty-four feet square is distributed equally to the four girders inclosing it, and in such a manner as to bear upon them at the points immediately over the vertical standards.

In the transverse direction of the building two pairs of joists, eight feet apart in each bay, are formed into trusses by tie-rods, $1\frac{3}{8}$ inches diameter, passed through a cast-iron shoe at each end, and pressing up two "struts," which are made to bear against the under-side of binding-timbers running longitudinally, or crossing the joists, and immediately under them. The cast-iron shoes for the trusses are bolted down to the girders, and serve at the same time to receive the standard supports of the gallery railing. The ends of the binding-timbers are secured by bolts and oak suspension-pieces to the other two girders inclosing the square. Joists about two feet six inches apart bear from girder to girder parallel to the trusses, and resting on the binding-timbers. On these is laid the floor, $1\frac{1}{4}$ inches thick, grooved and iron-tongued. A light cast-iron railing, forming a kind of trellis-work, is fixed between the columns, and is capped with a round mahogany hand-rail. From the view at page 60 the arrangement of the galleries will be readily understood.

TESTING THE CAST-IRON GIRDERS

ROM the very important office which the girders perform throughout the building, but more particularly those supporting the galleries, it was of the utmost importance that, previously to their being fixed in their places, the soundness of the casting should be proved; for it could hardly be expected that so large a number of girders could be produced without some of them being defective. The ordinary means of testing girders, by loading them with weights, would have occupied far too much time; and therefore an ingenious apparatus was devised by Mr. C. H. Wild for this purpose, by the use of which the testing of a girder occupied but a few minutes.

FRAME AND HYDRAULIC PRESS FOR TESTING THE GIRDERS.

It consisted of a very strong cast-iron frame rather longer than the girder, the bottom of which was formed by two fixed beams placed eight inches apart, and supported a few inches above the ground. At each end of these a cast-iron standard was firmly bolted between them and rose to a height rather greater than the depth of the girder to be tested; on the inner faces of these standards two "shoulders" were formed, which received the projections cast on the ends of the girder, as before mentioned. Between the fixed beams below, at two points dividing the whole length into three equal parts, were placed strong cylinders, with rising pistons connected with a forcing-pump, together with which they formed a Bramah's hydraulic press. A girder being placed in this frame, in an inverted position, the force applied by means of the pistons rising from the cylinders acted upon it precisely at those points, and in the same manner, as the load from the gallery or the roof would do when afterwards fixed in its place.

The essential parts of the Bramah's press may be thus briefly described. It consists of two cylinders, the diameter of one being considerably larger than that of the other. The smaller cylinder is fitted with a solid plunger or piston, by means of which water may be forced from it into the larger; this being also fitted with a rising piston, the force is communicated by it to the weight which it is desired to raise. The power obtained by means of this apparatus arises from the distributive power of fluids and the practical incompressibility of water, and it is proportioned to the difference of the diameters of the two cylinders; so that if a pressure of one pound per square inch be applied on the surface of the piston in the smaller cylinder, and the piston in the larger cylinder present a surface ten times greater, the power is multiplied by that number; whilst, in addition, the lever power used in applying the pressure to the smaller piston is obtained. The cylinders are fitted with valves, so arranged as to prevent the return of the water from the larger to the smaller, while the apparatus is in action, and thus the power is accumulated in the former.

In the instance before us, the two 3-inch cylinders already alluded to in the proving-frame took the place of the larger cylinder of the ordinary apparatus; and they were connected with the forcing-pump by a strong metal tube. When a girder had been fixed in the frame for proving, the force-pump was worked till the pistons underneath the girder carried it off its lower bearings and pressed it upwards against the "shoulders," by which it was firmly held, and the pressure was then continued until the amount previously fixed upon as necessary for proof had been obtained. This was ascertained by means of a self-adjusting apparatus attached to the hydraulic press.

An iron cylinder 1½ inches diameter was placed in communication with the pipe connecting the pump and the press, so that the pressure obtained in it was, in proportion to its diameter, the same as that in the large cylinder; and it was fitted with a piston-rod, working in a vertical direction. This piston-rod was connected with a lever, from the end of which a scale-pan was suspended, at a distance from the fulcrum ten times greater than that of the point of attachment of the piston from the same. The weight of the scale-pan and lever were balanced by a large mass of iron at the other end. In the scale-pan a certain weight was placed, proportioned to the proof desired to be obtained; and the action of the pump was continued until the water, rising in the iron cylinder just described, forced up the lever, and with it the weight attached; and thus indicated that the pressure to which it was desired to subject the girder had been reached. The weight to be placed in the scale-pan was thus determined: the diameter of the lever cylinder being 1½ inches, and that of each of those in the proving-frame three inches, the pistons or "rams" in the latter presented together eight times the surface of that in the lever cylinder; which being multiplied by the difference of length of the two parts of the lever, determines the weight for the scale-pan to be one-eightieth of that to which it was desired to prove the girder.

The ordinary gallery girders were tested with a pressure equivalent to a weight of fifteen tons; but it was calculated that, when fixed, the greatest weight they would have to sustain would be seven-and-a-half tons. In one instance, for the sake of experiment, the pressure was continued beyond the proof weight of fifteen tons, to see what amount of strain the girders would bear without fracture, and it was found that a strain of thirty tons produced no injurious effect; but the girder broke with an additional weight of half a ton.

ROOF OF TRANSEPT

E will now return to describe that portion of the roof which varies in form and arrangement from the rest, namely, the semicircular covering of the transept. This is supported by arched ribs, placed twenty-four feet apart, and constructed of Memel timber, in three thicknesses; the centre-piece four inches thick, with a 2-inch piece on each side of it. They are formed in lengths of about nine feet, placed so as to break joint; that is, the joints of the outer pieces fall upon the centre of the inner one. The thicknesses are fastened together by bolts passing through them about two feet six inches apart, besides being nailed at other points. On the inner circumference of the rib thus constructed there is then placed a piece of timber moulded to correspond with the form of the columns; and on the outer circumference two boards, each one inch thick, are bent round and attached to the rib with strong nails. On both the outer and inner circumference a flat bar of iron is secured by bolts passing through the whole depth of the rib, which, thus finished, measures eighteen inches in depth by eight inches in thickness. The ends of the ribs are fitted into sockets, formed by the upward continuation of the columns, to which they are attached by iron straps.

The ribs, which are supported by the trusses over the main avenue, have their ends bolted down upon a piece of timber secured on the upper portion of the truss; and they are further fixed in their places by oak brackets, forming a spreading foot on each side upon the same piece of timber.

Between these large ribs horizontal timbers, called "purlins," are fixed about nine feet apart, by means of cast-iron shoes, bolted both to them and to the ribs. These serve to support the minor or intermediate ribs, occurring at distances of eight feet apart; which consist of a single square piece of timber, having the two thicknesses of 1-inch board bent round their outer circumference, as on the main ribs. The boards form the gutters or furrows between which rise the ridges, in the same manner as in that portion of the roof which is horizontal.

The ridges, in this case, instead of being cut out of solid pieces, are formed in three thicknesses, bent round to the requisite curve, and so retained by small bolts tying them down to the "purlins." The sash-bars which receive the glass form, as elsewhere, the sloping rafters or supports of the ridge.

INTERIOR VIEW OF THE CENTRAL AVENUE TOWARDS THE WEST.

The space below the first "purlin" or plate at the springing of the arch, down to the level of the lead-flat beneath it, is fitted with louvre-frames for ventilation.

The diagonal bracing between the main ribs has been already alluded to. Each set consists of four wrought-iron rods three quarters of an inch in diameter, having eyes at one end, by means of which they are secured with bolts, passing through the thickness of the ribs; in the centre they meet in a cast-iron ring, on the inner side of which the ends are screwed up with nuts.

The semicircular ends of the transept are filled in with tracery, formed by radiating timbers, strutted apart with short pieces placed in concentric rings. The circular heads of the openings are formed by iron castings screwed into their places, and the eye from which the radiating lines of the tracery proceed is also formed by solid iron castings bolted together. On the outer face the ribs of the tracery are moulded, and on the inner side glazed sashes are fixed, filling in the openings.

The lead-flat, twenty-four feet wide, extending the whole length of the transept, on either side of the semicircular roof, is constructed in a similar manner to the floor of the galleries, by under-trussing two pairs of joists in each bay. In the width of the lead-flat roof a horizontal truss is formed by flat bars of iron fixed in the direction of the diagonal of the 24-feet square bays, to resist any possible thrust or tendency of the ends of the ribs to open outwards at the springing.

THE FACEWORK

THE external inclosures of the building, on the levels of the different storeys, require but little description in detail beyond that already given. The sash-bars dividing the sashes of the upper tiers are grooved for glass similarly to those used in the roof, and were cut out by the same machinery. The glass was put in after they were framed together, so that it was necessary to arrange the ends of the bars that it could be slipped in at one end. As the bars of these sashes were of slight dimensions and considerable length, they were strengthened by wrought-iron rods passed through the sash-frame and the bars, and screwed up at the ends, causing the whole to work together. The sashes are held in their position by small cast-iron clips, which are bolted on to the columns; and as the surface presented to the wind by the upright sides of the building is of such considerable extent, wooden bridges are fixed against the sashes on the inside, by small cast-iron shoes bolted to the columns; and at the internal angles, where the wind would exert its greatest force, these bridges are further strengthened by wrought-iron rods half an inch in diameter, pressing against the back of them, which is grooved for the purpose, and screwed up at each end in the cast-iron shoes. In this manner a connected chain of resistance to any external pressure is established round the whole circuit of the building.

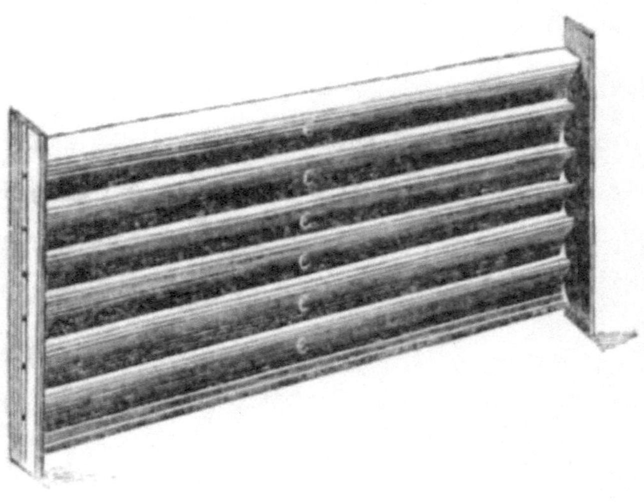

THE LOUVRE-FRAME.

The louvre-frames, which form part of the face-work in all the different storeys, consist of a deal frame in which bent louvre-blades are hung on pivots at each end. These blades are of galvanised iron of an **S** form. On the back of each blade is fixed a loop of thin iron, to which a rack is   fitted; and by these means all the blades in each frame are moved simultaneously. A considerable number of these racks may also be connected, so that a large area of ventilation may be regulated at once.

THE DIAGONAL BRACING

ROM the total absence in this building of any internal division-walls, which in ordinary structures considerably add to their stability, it was thought desirable to introduce into the construction something to compensate for this deficiency. At several points in the length of the building, where a continuous connexion could be established transversely, the squares formed by the columns and girders on the different storeys have their four corners connected by diagonal rods, seven-eighths of an inch in diameter, having eyes at the ends, by which they are secured to the bolts connecting the different parts of the columns. In the centre of the square the four rods meet in a cast-iron ring, and are screwed up with nuts; ornamental faces are fitted into the rings, so that this addition to the construction is by no means detrimental to the general effect.

In a similar manner this diagonal bracing is introduced in a horizontal direction immediately under the floor of some portions of the galleries; of these there are twenty-two sets, and of those placed vertically there are, altogether, 220 sets in the building, and the manner of their introduction will be readily understood from the views of the interior.

THE STAIRCASES

HE double staircases, of which it has been mentioned there are eight in the building, consist each of four flights, about eight feet wide; two parallel ones, leading from the ground-floor to a landing, at the half-height, and the other two branching in opposite directions from the landing to the two galleries. The treads of the steps are made of a species of mahogany called sabicu, which is much harder than oak, and therefore peculiarly suited to the purpose for which it is here employed. The risers, or faces of the steps, are of deal. The stairs are supported by cast-iron girders, following the slope, the lower ones being fixed at the foot to stout timbers under the flooring, and the upper ends bolted to the cast-iron columns which support the landing. These columns are of the same pattern as the rest throughout the building, but only five inches in diameter. They are supported on concrete, and eight of them are required for each staircase. The floor of the landing is carried by lesser cast-iron girders, with flooring-joists.

The girders carrying the upper flights spring from the landing girders, and have their upper ends bolted on to the main girders supporting the galleries, which are varied in pattern for this purpose. The railing of the staircase is formed in separate cast-iron standards, one to each step, which are bolted on to the top flange of the girders; and the foot of the standard is so continued that the ends of the treads are fitted into it, and are thus supported. The pattern of these standards is assimilated to that of the gallery railing.

The hand-rail is formed of Honduras mahogany, with carved ends. On each side of the upper flight, which occupies the centre of a 24-feet space, connecting-galleries about eight feet wide are carried, establishing a communication between the two lines of gallery without descending to the level of the landing and then re-ascending. The landing is sufficiently high above the ground-floor to give ample headway for passing underneath it; so that the space occupied by the staircases on the ground-floor is but small.

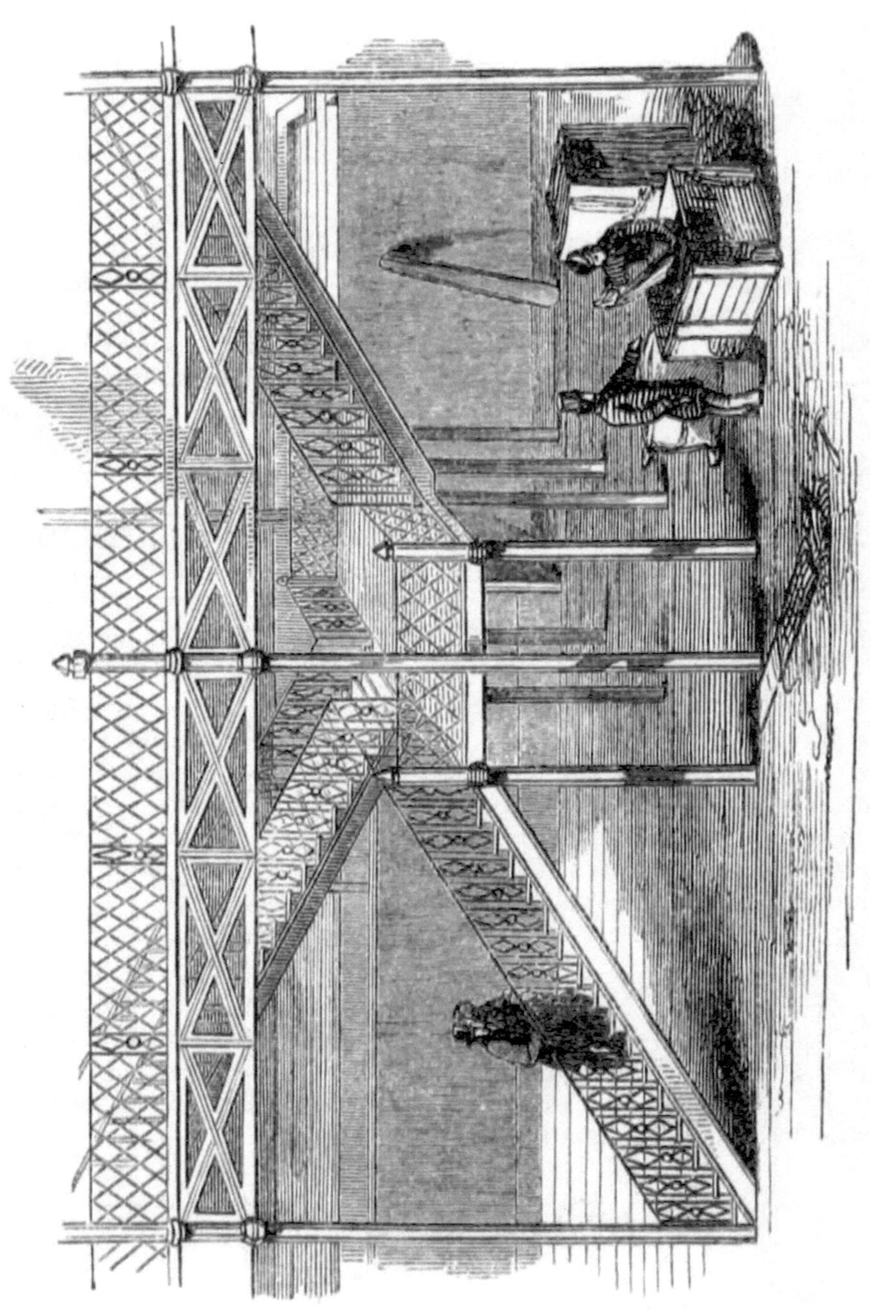

VIEW OF STAIRCASE.

THE FLOOR AND FOUNDATIONS

T now only remains to mention briefly the construction of the floor of the building, and the foundations for the base-pieces. The substratum of the site consists of gravel of an excellent quality, and sufficiently dense to have sustained, perhaps without any preparation, the load brought upon it by the bases of the columns. A thickness of concrete, proportioned in all cases to the amount of the weight to be borne by the superincumbent columns, and of such a size as to be two feet in each direction larger than the bed-plates, was placed upon the gravel, and the upper surface was finished with a bed of fine mortar to receive the bed-plates. In this manner it was calculated that in no case would a greater weight than two-and-a-half tons be borne by each foot superficial of the gravel—previous experiments having shown that a considerably larger weight could be placed upon it without any injurious effect.

The timbers supporting the joists for the floor are also placed upon small blocks of concrete, about one foot cube, at a distance of eight feet apart. On these are fixed the flooring-joists, and a deal floor an inch and a half thick is laid on them, as has been already mentioned, with intervals of about half an inch between the boards.

FIXING CAST-IRON DRAIN-PIPE.

In order to carry off the water brought down from the roof by every alternate longitudinal row of columns, 6-inch cast-iron pipes are fitted into the sockets described in the base-pieces, and are carried in the lines of those columns through the whole length of the building, with discharges into the larger drains at the centre and at each end; the natural slope of the ground gives a sufficient fall to the pipes.

Having thus described in detail all the different portions of the construction of the building, we must proceed to give some account of its actual erection, which will enable us to mention many very ingenious mechanical contrivances which were employed in the course of its progress.

FIRST OPERATIONS ON THE GROUND

ROM the great extent of the area required for the building, it was not to be expected that any site would be found of the necessary size, perfectly level. On the ground occupied by the building there is a difference of level between the two extreme ends of about eight feet. In consequence of this fall of the natural surface from west to east, and in order to avoid having a considerable flight of steps at one end of the building to compensate for it, it was determined to arrange the floor with an inclination following nearly that of the ground, such fall being at the rate of one inch in twenty-four feet. All the lines of the building which would be called horizontal in fact follow this line of the floor, and those which are supposed to be upright are placed at right angles to the floor, and therefore slightly inclined from the perpendicular towards the east. The deviation, however, is so exceedingly small as to be perfectly imperceptible even to those who are aware of the fact; and no one who was not previously informed of it would be able to detect it.

It has been mentioned that Messrs. Fox and Henderson's tender for the building was verbally accepted on the 16th of July, 1850, and on the 30th of that month they obtained possession of the site from the Commissioners of Woods and Forests.

The first proceeding was to inclose the whole area (including a considerable space at each end more than would be covered by the building) with a hoarding about eight feet high, put together in a very simple manner, so that the boards were afterwards available for the flooring. The supports for the hoarding consisted of pieces of timber fixed in the ground in pairs, at intervals of the length of the boards, leaving a narrow space between them, into which the boards were dropped, and thus held in their place without any nails. Temporary offices were then erected in a convenient portion of the site, and were covered with a roofing which was a specimen of that to be used in the building itself. Considerable ranges of carpenters' sheds were also put up, and even stables for twenty or thirty horses, which were required in the progress of the works.

SETTING-OUT THE GROUND

HE first thing to be done towards the building itself was to set out accurately all the points where the columns would stand, as well as the general outline of the building. It will be readily understood that this was an exceedingly important part of the work, as upon its accuracy depended the fitting together of the various parts that had afterwards to be put in place.

This part of the work was executed with great precision by Mr. W. G. Brounger. He commenced by determining the four extreme angles of the building, and the centre lines of the main avenues. These formed fixed points from which were determined the whole of the centres for the columns.

Our readers will recollect that the dimension of twenty-four feet occurs horizontally throughout the building, either in multiples or sub-multiples. In order to measure off the different distances, rods of American pine were made, into which, near the ends, pieces of metal were fixed, having corresponding notches at the exact distance of twenty-four feet apart. By these means the lengths were measured off with great accuracy, as the wood used is not liable to alteration in the length of its fibre; and by means of the metal notches the rods were sure to be placed correctly together. It was necessary to make these sockets or notches of metal, from the great amount of work the rods had to perform.

In determining the length of the rods, the standard of the Astronomical Society was used; and this was referred to in all important measurements for the castings and other parts of the building, to insure their precise eventual agreement in length. This will hardly be considered to have been unnecessary when it is remembered that, from the great length of the building, a very minute error in any of the parts would have been so multiplied as sensibly to throw out the ends.

To those who are unacquainted with the fact, it may be well to mention that the standard of length referred to is obtained from a pendulum, which oscillates seconds, in the latitude of London, in a vacuum, at the level of the sea, at a certain fixed temperature. The length of this pendulum is then divided into a certain registered number of feet and inches.

The rods above described were carried along the centre lines of the columns, and the position of each column was marked by a small stake driven into the ground; and in order still more accurately to fix the centre, a long nail was driven into the head of the stake. In this manner the position of every column throughout the building was determined.

The level at which the floor was to be fixed was the next point determined by the ordinary method of levelling, and stakes, with a **T** piece at the top, called boning-sticks, were fixed in different parts of the building; by the aid of which the tops of the base-pieces for the columns were all afterwards fixed in one plane of the required slope.

FIXING THE BASE-PLATES

HE next proceeding was to excavate the holes for the concrete, on which the base-pieces were to stand. To do this, the stakes marking the centres of the columns had to be removed, and it was therefore necessary to adopt some method of finding those centres again with precision. For this purpose a large carpenter's square, as it is called, was made. This instrument forms a right-angled triangle, and in this instance was used in the following manner:—The centre of its longest side, or hypothenuse, was marked by a line, which, if continued, would pass through the right angle of the triangle, and at an equal distance along each of the other sides of the triangle from the right angle an upright saw-cut or notch was made. The square was then placed horizontally, so that the line marked on the hypothenuse coincided with that of the centres of a row of columns, and so that the right-angled corner of the square touched the nail marking the exact site of a column. Two small stakes were then driven under the notches in the short arms of the square, and nails were driven into them through the notches. It will be seen that by these means the site of the first stake could easily be again ascertained after its removal. The holes for the concrete were then dug of an oval form and of the various sizes and depths required, and the concrete filled in to the proper height. The gravel used for the concrete was raised in a pit at one end of the ground.

Next to the setting out of the positions of the columns, perhaps the operation of fixing the base-pieces was that in which the greatest accuracy was required; for as there were in some parts three storeys of columns to be fixed over them, any inaccuracy as to their level or position would be very much increased at the top of the building. To fix the base-pieces over the centres that had been determined for the columns, another carpenter's square was made use of, like that already described, but having the right-angled corner cut out to the form of the section of a column. This square being placed with the notches in its short sides over the two stakes already described, the upright portion of the base-piece was fitted into the notch at the angle; and as the reader will at once see, if he has followed us in the description of the various processes, its correct position was thus exactly found.

In order to determine the level of the top of the base-pieces, boning-sticks were placed in the lines of the columns, and when the base-piece had been approximately fixed, a piece of wood was placed on it edgeways, the top of which was to range with the top of the boning-sticks. This was easily arranged by looking along them; and the workmen drove down the base-piece with a wooden mallet till the desired level was obtained.

From what has been previously stated, it may be gathered that the base-pieces had to be fixed truly upright in one direction, but slightly inclined in the other; and to effect this a plumb-rule was made, on which the deviation from the perpendicular line was marked; and this, when applied to those faces of the base-pieces which were to incline, served to show when the proper inclination was arrived at, whilst an ordinary plumb-rule applied to the other upright faces tested their vertical position.

The first column was raised on the ground on the 26th of September, but little more than two months after the tender had been accepted. In the meantime, many of the different castings had already arrived on the ground, and a considerable advance had been made in the carpenter's work for the gutters and other parts. The semi-circular ribs for the transept roof were also being put together, and stacked in such a manner as not to stand in the way of the other works.

VIEW OF CRANE AND PROVING-PRESS.

We may mention here that every casting, as it came on to the ground, was weighed and registered, and every girder proved, as already described; in doing which considerable assistance was derived from one of Mr. Henderson's patent Derrick cranes, which was erected near the proving-apparatus. By its means a girder was raised from the waggon in which it arrived, placed on the weighing-machine, weighed, removed to the proving-press, tested, raised again, and deposited on the ground in a stack, in less than four minutes.

HENDERSON'S DERRICK CRANE

(Fig. 1.)

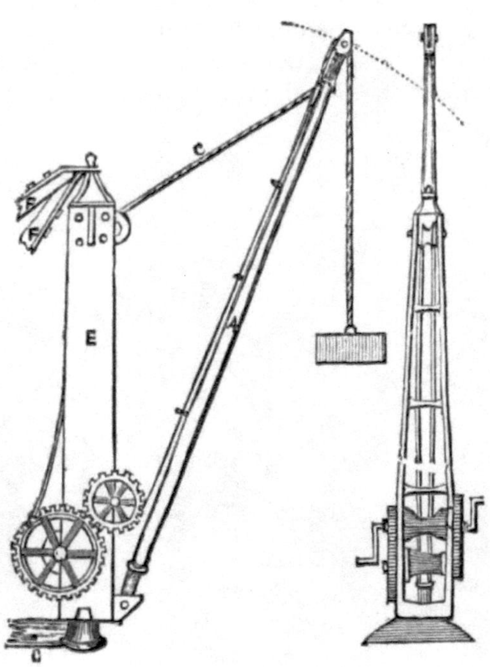

HENDERSON'S DERRICK CRANE.

(Fig. 2.)

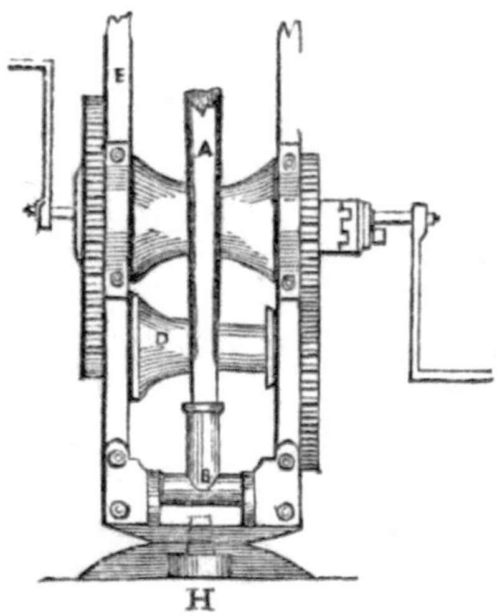

PART OF HENDERSON'S DERRICK CRANE.

(Fig. 3.)

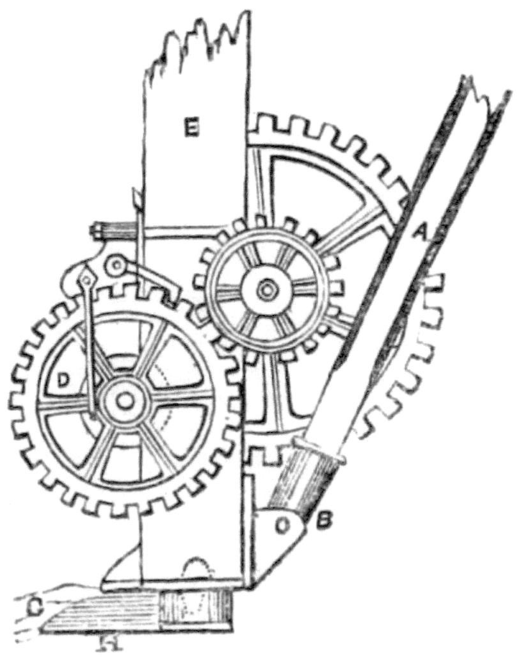

PART OF HENDERSON'S DERRICK CRANE.

BRIEF description of this useful engine may not be out of place here. It consists of an upright mast (E), steadied when the crane is in use by two sloping stays (F F). These stays are fixed into horizontal timbers (G) on the ground, connected with the foundation-plate (H) on which the mast turns. At the foot of the mast is fixed a combination of wheels and working handles for raising the weight, technically called a crab. A beam (A) working at the bottom in a socket (B, Fig. 3) fixed to the foot of the mast, but hanging out from it in a sloping direction, is called the DERRICK, and forms the principal peculiarity of the crane, as it can be raised more to the upright line, or lowered to slope more outwards, as may be desired, by means of the chain (C). The advantage of this is obvious; for a weight may thus be raised from or deposited at any point within a circle of a certain radius, depending on the length of the derrick; whereas, in an ordinary crane, the weight can only be placed at points upon the circumference of that circle. The whole engine revolves on a pivot (H, Fig. 2) at the foot of the mast. Cranes of this description are made varying in power from one to forty tons, and with derricks ranging from twenty to sixty feet radius.

RAISING AND FIXING THE COLUMNS AND GIRDERS

MANY of the persons who visited the building during the progress of its erection were heard to inquire "where was the scaffolding;" and others even imagined that the skeleton framework they saw was, in fact, only the scaffolding for the building, and not parts of its actual construction. This leads us to point out one of the most interesting peculiarities of the structure; namely, that it formed, as it were, the scaffolding for its own erection. In order to raise the columns upon the base-pieces, two poles were placed upright, connected by a horizontal piece, forming what is called shear-legs; the whole being steadied in its position by ropes from the summit fixed to the ground in various directions. A rope with pulleys fixed to the horizontal piece served to hoist the column, and sustain it in a vertical position until the bolts were passed through the projecting rings at the bottom of the column and the corresponding ones at the top of the base-piece, and screwed up. When two columns had been thus fixed, a connecting-piece was attached to each end of a girder, and the whole raised by the same apparatus, and fixed on the top of the columns; bolts being passed through the holes in the projections of the connecting-pieces, corresponding with those on the top of the columns. The shear-legs were then moved on twenty-four feet to perform the same duties to another pair of columns; and two sides of a 24-feet bay were thus formed. To complete the square, two more girders were raised in a similar manner, and fixed between the connecting-pieces over the columns. The square bay then became a firm structure, requiring no further support; and by repeating these operations all the smaller avenues of the building were erected, of the different heights of one, two, or three storeys. The greatest number of columns thus fixed in one week was 310.

FIXING THE GIRDERS.

GENERAL VIEW OF THE WORKS IN PROGRESS.

HOISTING THE ROOF TRUSSES

HE wrought-iron roof-trusses over the 48-feet avenues were raised in a similar manner to the columns and girders; and in all cases horses were employed to run out the end of the fall-rope, which was passed through a pulley or catch-block at the foot of the shear-legs, in order to change its direction from vertical to horizontal.

For raising the roof-trusses of seventy-two feet span over the main avenue a somewhat different method was employed. A single mast or derrick, more than seventy feet high, was placed in the centre of the avenue, and steadied in an upright position by guide-ropes spreading from the top in various directions. Near its summit the hoisting-tackle was firmly lashed on. The trusses to be hoisted were brought from the places where they had been put together, and placed across the main avenue at the points where they were to be fixed. Two ends of a stout chain were passed round the upper portion of the truss, at points dividing its length into about three equal parts. To this chain the hoisting-tackle was attached, guide-ropes being further fastened to each end of the truss to steady it in its ascent. In order to stiffen the truss horizontally, struts were attached at the centre projecting on each side, and held in their place by tie-rods attached to the upper part of the truss, and forming a triangle on each side. Before the truss, therefore, could bend in a horizontal direction, the attachment of these tie-rods must have given way. Six horses drew out the end of the fall-rope, and in the course of a very few minutes the truss was hoisted to its giddy height, and each end slipped in between the projections made in the connecting-pieces to receive it.

The animated scene presented by these operations was highly interesting from the number of men employed, both on the ground and for fixing the trusses in their position aloft, and from the rapid progress so many hands made. Each gang of men was managed by a foreman, who was obliged to issue his orders through a speaking-trumpet, to enable his voice to be heard in the din caused by the other works going on around. Besides the two large gangs of men engaged in the hoisting of the trusses, other smaller gangs were at work at different points getting up the columns and girders. In one part, the roofing of which was completed as early as practicable, a crowd of carpenters were preparing the Paxton's gutters and other portions of the work. In another place, as soon as a sufficient space could be roofed over and a temporary floor laid, various parts of the machinery we have already described were fitted up and worked by portable steam-engines. Of these there were three in different parts: one drove the machinery for finishing the sash-bars, gutters, ridges, &c.; another worked the drilling, punching, and other machinery connected with the iron-work; and a third was used for working circular saws.

Of the number of trusses that were hoisted as above described, in only one instance (and that the first) was the result otherwise than perfectly successful. The first truss was raised by its ends, instead of from the centre; but that method was afterwards abandoned, from the difficulty of maintaining the truss in an upright position during its ascent; which was important, as, if it turned on its side, its lateral strength was not sufficient to prevent it from bending, which would have destroyed the joints of the work.

One of the tall masts was worked on each side of the transept, from the centre to the ends of the building, being maintained constantly in an upright position, while traversing from point to point, by alternate slackening and hauling up of the ropes which steadied it; and it was curious to witness the motion of these tall giants, as they slowly progressed from one point to another, in the performance of their important office. Stout planks were laid along the ground, upon which the foot of the mast was forced forward by crowbars and levers; the planks served also to distribute the weight, which would otherwise have sunk the end into the ground. As many as seven trusses were hoisted in one day by each derrick, which had therefore to travel a distance of 168 feet.

So careful were the men, under the direction of the manager (to whom was intrusted the active superintendence of the whole erection of the building), that no accident of importance occurred in these difficult operations.

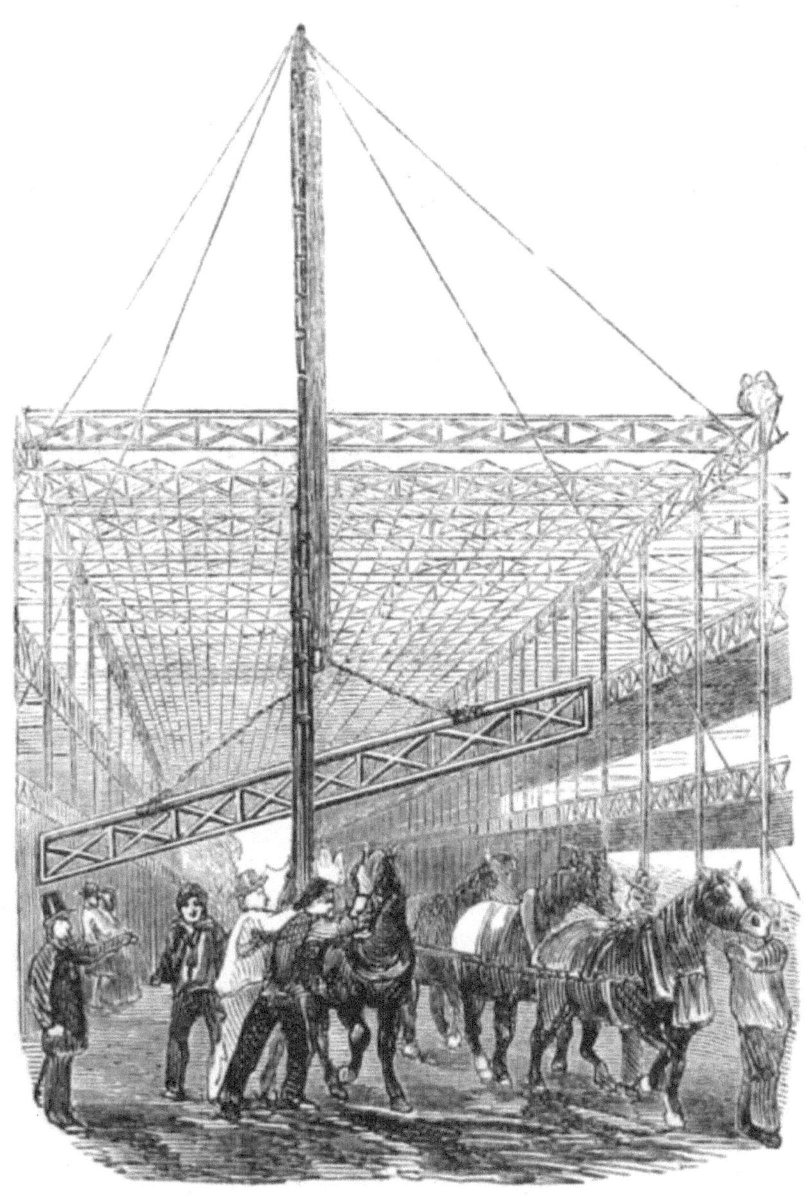

HOISTING THE 72-FEET TRUSSES.

PROVISION FOR EXPANSION OF GIRDERS

N connexion with the fixing of the girders, it may be desirable to mention the provision that was made for the expansion and contraction of the iron, which in so great a length as that of the building might have otherwise produced results prejudicial to its stability.

Between the projections cast on to the connecting-pieces and those projecting from the ends of the girders which they were made to clip, sufficient space was left for the introduction of oak keys, by driving in which the girder was fixed in its place, whilst the compressibility of the wood left sufficient play for the expansion of the metal. In describing the girders, it was mentioned that in the upper and lower flat flanges small sinkings were cast near the ends. Corresponding with these sinkings, a notch was left in the projection which came out from the connecting-piece; and when the girder was put into its place, iron wedges were driven in between the notch and the sinking, by which means any lateral motion of the girder was prevented. It was a great advantage to have the means of fixing the girders of so simple a nature, as any arrangement presenting the least complication, or requiring great nicety, would have materially retarded the progress of the work.

The wrought-iron trusses were held by the connecting-pieces in a similar manner to the cast-iron girders; but, as an additional security, bolts were passed through holes provided in the standards at the ends, and through the connecting-pieces, where they were screwed up with nuts.

The raising and fixing of the extra-strong roof-trusses crossing the main avenue near the side of the transept required particular care, from their great weight; the heaviest being, as we have before mentioned, no less than eight tons. These trusses were the first that were fixed across the central avenue, and about 150 men were engaged in the hoisting of each one. They are secured to the columns by four strong bolts passing through the end-standards.

In order to provide additional support for the great weight brought upon the last-mentioned trusses by the transept roof, extra columns were introduced underneath them. These were built up in storeys corresponding with those of the other columns, with which they were connected, at the levels of the girders, by bolts and straps. A cast-iron shoe, fixed on the top of the columns, provided a bearing for the ends of the truss. The columns just described project slightly into the main avenue from the line of the other columns; and this is the only instance in the interior of the building of the iron columns occurring at a less distance than twenty-four feet apart.

GLAZING THE ROOF

E have now traced the erection of the building up to the level of the roof, in which it will be readily conceived the operation of glazing was one of extreme difficulty, there being no scaffolding to aid the workmen in conducting their operations. When the glazing was first commenced a light scaffolding was suspended from the rafters; but this was found to be too tedious and troublesome a method of proceeding for so large an extent of roofing. It was, moreover, of great importance that some means should be devised for completing this part of the construction independently of the weather; a matter of some moment, when it is remembered that the work had to be done in the winter, when in our climate such operations are liable to be very much impeded by heavy rain. The arrangements made to meet this difficulty, as well as some others for carrying on the works, are very clearly described in a paper by Mr. Digby Wyatt, read at the Institution of Civil Engineers, on the 14th January, 1851, from which we quote some passages, by permission, for the benefit of our readers.

With reference to the means employed for glazing the roof he says: "To effect this purpose, a travelling stage was devised by Mr. Fox, which superseded the necessity of any scaffolding for glazing, and by means of seventy-six of these machines nearly the whole of the work has been executed. The stage was about eight feet square, and rested on four small wheels travelling in the Paxton's gutters. It thus embraced a width of one bay of eight feet of the roof, with one ridge and two sloping sides. Each bay in width required, therefore, a separate stage."

"Each stage was occupied by two workmen, and was covered by an awning of canvass stretched over hoops, to protect them in bad weather, and was further provided with a box on each side to contain a supply of glass. The sash-bars and other materials were piled upon the stage itself, the centre of the platform being left open for the convenience of hoisting up materials, for which purpose there was a small iron arm with a single block pulley."

GLAZING-WAGGON, FOR FLAT ROOF.

"Whilst working, the men sat at one end of the platform (the ridge having been previously fixed in position by means of the extra-strong sash-bars), and they fixed the glass in front of them, pushing the stage backwards as they completed each pane. On coming to the strong sash-bars previously fixed, they temporarily removed them to allow the stage to pass. In this manner each stage travelled, uninterruptedly, from the transept to the east and west ends of the building, and the glaziers were enabled to follow up the previously-fixed work very closely. The average amount of glazing done by one man per day was fifty-eight squares, or about 200 superficial feet; and the largest amount done by any one man in a working-day was 108 squares, or 367 superficial feet."

The mode of fixing the squares of glass was this: a sash-bar having been nailed down between the ridge and the gutter, the workman inserted one long edge of a square of glass into the groove in the sash-bar, he then placed a loose bar against the other long edge of the glass and brought the whole down to bear upon the ridge and gutter, the second sash-bar fitting into the notches prepared for it; the glass was then pressed up a little, in order to insert its upper edge into the groove in the ridge, and the workman then filled in the grooves on the outside of the glass with putty, the lower edge of the glass having been also bedded on putty where it bears on the edge of the gutter. The ends of each sash-bar were fixed with a nail driven into the holes previously drilled.

STAGE FOR REPAIRING THE GLASS, ETC.

S it might naturally be expected that out of the thousands of panes of glass employed, particularly in the flat roof of the building, many would be broken in the course of the works, subsequently to their being fixed, it was necessary that a ready means should be devised for repairing any such damage, as the glazing-waggons used for the first execution of the work would not be available for that purpose. A light stage was therefore constructed, travelling with wooden wheels upon the ridges instead of in the gutters; and from this the men were able to perform their work without walking along the narrow gutters, which would have been attended with much risk. This stage was also used for fixing the canvass on the outside of the roofing, where it is nailed along the ridges, and allowed to bag down slightly between them. The object of the canvass, which covers externally the whole of the roof except the transept, is twofold: it preserves the glass from damage, and also protects the objects exhibited from the direct rays of the sun, which would, of course, in many instances, be very prejudicial; for the latter purpose the upright sashes on the south side are also covered with canvass on the inside.

HOISTING THE RIBS FOR TRANSEPT ROOF

NE of the most interesting operations which attracted the attention of the numerous visitors to the works was the raising the ribs for the semicircular roof of the transept, the description of which we give from Mr. Wyatt's paper:—

"The operation about which most anxiety had been felt was the hoisting of the arched ribs of the transept. These ribs were constructed on the ground horizontally, and when completed with all their bolts, two of them were reared on end, and maintained in a vertical position, at a distance of twenty-four feet from each other, by guy-ropes. As the ribs singly possessed little lateral stiffness, they were framed together in pairs with the purlins, intermediate small ribs and diagonal tie-rods, forming a complete bay of the roof twenty-four feet long; two complete sets of temporary ties were also introduced to provide for the strains incident to the variations in position of the ribs during the hoisting. The feet of the ribs were bolted on to a stout piece of timber, and the lower purlins strutted up from the same." In this state the framework is shown in the engraving.

A PAIR OF RIBS PREPARED FOR RAISING.

"The whole framework was then moved on rollers to the centre of the square formed by the intersection of the transept and the main avenue, where it was afterwards hoisted. All the ribs were landed over this square, and were afterwards moved on a tramway formed of a half baulk of timber constructed over the columns on either side of the transept, at a height of about four feet above the lead-flat. The hoisting-tackle consisted of four crabs, each one being placed on the side of the transept opposite to the part of the ribs to be lifted by it, so that the men at the crabs might watch the effect of their exertions with greater convenience."

"The hoisting-shears were placed on the lead-flat immediately over the deep trusses of seventy-two feet span; each set consisted of three stout scaffold-poles, lashed together at the top, and footed on planks laid across the flat, and secured by the necessary guy-ropes. The hoisting-rope passed from each of the crabs across the transept horizontally, to a leading block attached to the foot of the opposite angle column of the square; it then passed up to a treble block fastened to the shears on the flat, and from thence down to a double block secured by chains to the bottom part of the ribs."

HOISTING THE RIBS FOR THE TRANSEPT ROOF.

"There was a peculiar difficulty to be overcome in this operation, which arose from the circumstance that the width of the framework was greater than that of the transept, the extreme width of the framework to be hoisted being seventy-four feet, and the clear width apart of the trusses above which it had to be hoisted being only seventy-one feet four inches. It was therefore necessary to raise one side to a height of thirty-five feet before raising the other, so as to diminish the horizontal width of the whole, the diameter of the semicircle being maintained at this angle; the whole was then hoisted, until the highest end could clear the tramway."

This accounts for the slanting position in which the ribs are shown in the view given.

"The foot of the ribs on one side was then passed over the tramway sufficiently to allow the other side to clear the opposite truss; after which the whole was hoisted to the full height, and rested on rollers of hard wood placed between the sills attached to the framework and the tramway, by means of which it was moved to its permanent position. There it was again raised by another set of shears, while the sill and tramway were removed from under it; and the ribs were then lowered into the sockets prepared for them, formed by the continuation of the columns above the level of the lead-flat."

"Each successive pair of ribs was fixed at a distance of twenty-four feet, or one bay from the preceding one; and the purlins, &c., were fixed in the intervening space without any scaffolding from the ground, by means of jointed ladders, which were adjusted to the form of the roof."

The first pair of ribs was hoisted December 4th, and the eighth pair on December 12th. The operation, which was one of great excitement and considerable anxiety, was personally superintended by the contractors, aided by their most able foremen and assistants; and a crowd of visitors, including many of the illustrious promoters of the undertaking, watched with intense interest the steady ascent of the apparently unwieldy piece of construction, and every spectator seemed astonished at the mechanical regularity with which the whole operation proceeded. It took about one hour to raise a pair from the ground to the level of the lead-flat, and the whole was done without any accident whatever. About sixty men were employed in the hoisting, there being eleven men to each crab, and the remainder on the lead-flats.

GLAZING THE TRANSEPT ROOF

HE semicircular form of the transept roof rendered it necessary to adopt a different mode of operation for glazing it to that used in the horizontal portion. A stage, thirty-two feet long and about three feet wide, with a protecting rail at the side, was constructed, so that it rested upon rollers, travelling on the ridges. It was slung by ropes from the crown of the arched roof, and could be raised and lowered at pleasure. It accommodated eight workmen, with the necessary quantity of materials in sash-bars and glass; and they thus performed, with ease and rapidity, an operation which before the fitting-up of the stage appeared at least extremely difficult, and to the uninitiated next to impossible.

STAGE FOR GLAZING THE ROOF OF TRANSEPT.

The men commenced fixing the glass at the bottom or springing of the arch, and as they completed their work the stage was raised at intervals by labourers stationed on the lead-flat. A portion of the glazing at the crown of the arch was effected by men working on a light scaffold, suspended within from the temporary ties mentioned as having been attached to the ribs; whilst those upon the stage worked upwards till they joined the portion done from the top.

THE PAINTING

PORTION of the work which necessarily occupied a very large amount of time was the painting, which was necessary for the preservation of all the parts, as well as for their appearance; and when it is considered that every portion required to be gone over four times, it must be evident that it was highly desirable to adopt some means for facilitating the operation. It was found that the sash-bars of the roof, being in short lengths and of small dimensions, could readily be operated upon by some mechanical contrivance.

THE SASH-BAR PAINTING-MACHINE.

A wooden trough was made sufficiently long to receive the sash-bars, and this was filled with paint; a number of the bars were then put into it, and upon being taken out separately, they were passed through a frame into which a set of brushes were fixed in such a manner as to clear off all the unnecessary paint. Two small brushes, placed where the bar first entered the frame, cleared out the grooves. One workman pushed the bar in at one end of the frame, which was about two feet six inches long, and another drew it out at the other end, where a trough was placed to receive any droppings of paint. The bars were then stacked upright, until they were sufficiently dry for the next coat. The first coat only was put on by this apparatus, the second being done in the ordinary manner, and the last not till after the work was all fixed in its place. By means of this apparatus a workman could perform at least ten times the amount of work done in the ordinary way.

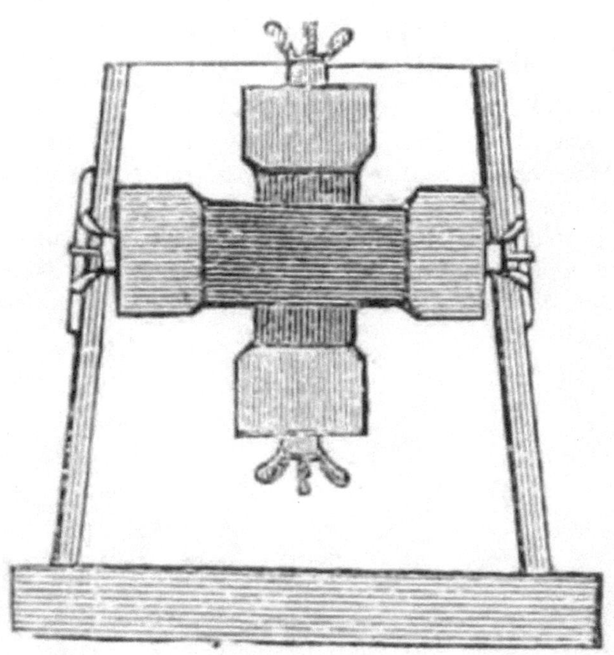

THE FRAME-WORK WITH BRUSHES.

The finishing the painting of the various parts of the roof internally, after they had been put together, was very ingeniously managed, so that while the workmen were able to work with ease to themselves, the scaffolding on which they stood required no supports from the ground, where they would have been much in the way of other operations; loops of wrought-iron were hooked on to the roof-trusses, and by means of these a perfect cloud of scaffold-boards was suspended, enabling between 400 and 500 men to be at work at one time. The roof of the main avenue, particularly, presented a very singular appearance, as nearly one half of the entire length was thus covered at one time, and a crowd of painters were at work over the heads of many, perhaps unconscious exhibitors, who were arranging their goods undisturbed below.

THE HAND-RAIL MACHINE

NE of the mechanical contrivances which were put up on the ground during the works, for saving labour and increasing the rapidity of production, remains to be mentioned; it was contrived for turning out the rounded mahogany hand-rail for the gallery railing as well as that for the staircases.

The mahogany being supplied in slabs of the requisite thickness, these were first cut up by circular saws into pieces of a square section, and the angles of these were then bevelled off by the same means; the lengths were afterwards transferred to the hand-rail cutting machine to be rounded.

THE HAND-RAIL CUTTING MACHINE.

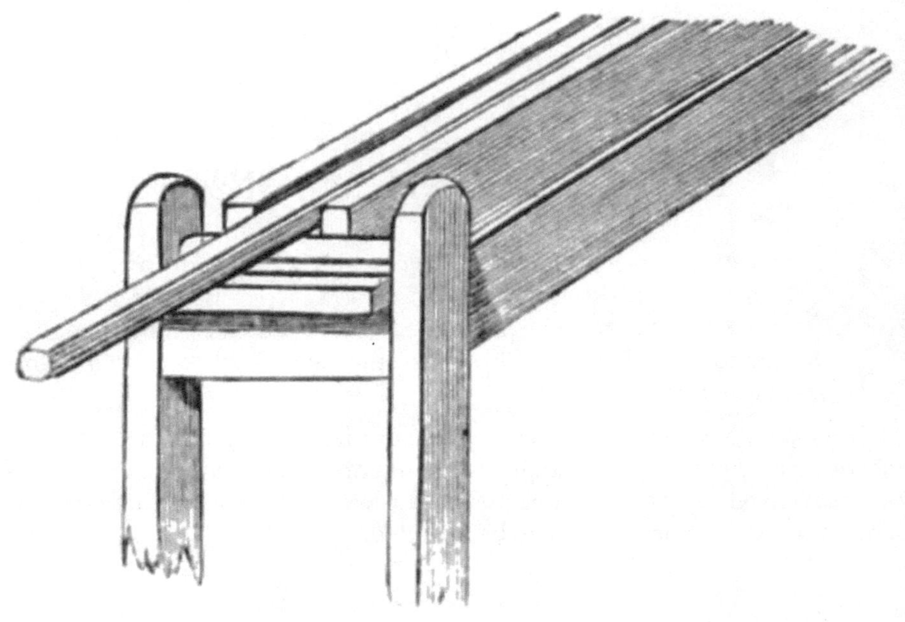

PART OF HAND-RAIL MACHINE.

The principal portion of the machine consists of a hollow cast-iron cylinder, round which a strap may be passed to drive it. At one end of this cylinder four cutters are fixed, so that a piece of wood passing between them and through the cylinder, as it revolves, is rounded off to a true circular form of section, and is turned out so smoothly finished as to require scarcely any further work upon it before fixing. In advance of the cutters pressure-rollers are placed, furnished with teeth; and these, as they are turned round by a cranked handle, seize upon a piece of mahogany and force it forward against the cutters, which form, as it were, the jaws of the hollow cylinder, which thus seems to be constantly swallowing lengths of rough mahogany, which escape from it finished. The wooden rail is passed up to the cutters along a groove, the end of which is shown in the small engraving; and opposite each end of the revolving cylinder springs are fixed, which prevent the rail from shifting its position. The hand-rail was all turned out in 21-feet lengths, of which about thirty were completed in the day.

GENERAL VIEW OF THE WORKS

E have mentioned that the actual commencement of the building was made by fixing one of the columns on the 26th of September; and, within a few weeks, more than a thousand men were at work, though, from the great extent of the ground they were spread over, it was difficult to estimate their number, which was, however, made apparent by the rapidity with which the building began to grow. The place presented an animated and interesting scene, which attracted a great number of visitors; and crowds of the fair sex were not deterred by the rough state of the ground from endeavouring to satisfy their proverbial thirst for knowledge. In one part of the ground might be seen the putting together of the wrought-iron roof-girders to the deafening tune of more than a hundred hammers; in another place gutters were being put together by the mile, for which some hundred or two of sawyers were cutting up ship-loads of timber. Three portable steam-engines in various parts were driving the different machinery already described, which, however, was mostly grouped in one place near the transept. The central avenue formed, of course, the great thoroughfare, where teams of horses were constantly passing, dragging the slender columns, or unwieldy-looking girders, to their places, while other teams were engaged in running them up to their final position. Over-head, too, the glaziers' waggons, dotted about the roof, seemed to be running on some new aerial railways; in every direction that the eye turned the busy scene extended.

For carrying on these extensive works an immense number of men were necessarily employed on the spot, besides those occupied in preparing the various parts at different places. The greatest number of men on the ground in any one week was 2,260; and the season of the year frequently rendered it necessary for the workmen to continue their labours after dark, which they did partly by the light of huge bonfires of shavings and odd scraps of wood. The effect of these great fires, which were generally lighted in some part of the main avenue, was exceedingly grand. The light of the tall flames was reflected from the glass of the roof far away into the darkness which concealed all the other parts; whilst occasionally a lantern carried by a workman engaged in fixing the upper columns, or some part of the roof, glimmered like some new star.

On one occasion, when the greatest efforts were being made to push on the progress of the works, no less than twelve large bonfires lighted the men at their midnight toil; and had the building been formed of combustible materials, a passing observer would have imagined that the whole was in flames.

PAYING THE WORKMEN

HE process of distributing their wages among so large a number of men, on every recurring Saturday evening, was one which could only be effected within a reasonable time by some systematic arrangement; and to such perfection was this brought in the course of the works, that the whole number of 2,000 men or upwards were sometimes paid in little more than an hour; though at first it occupied a considerably longer time.

The mode in which this was effected was as follows:—When a workman was engaged his name was entered in a book against a certain number, which was stamped on several brass tickets, three of which were given to each workman before leaving the ground in the evening.

THE BRASS TICKETS AND MONEY-BOX.

Every man had to enter the premises three times in the course of the day; namely, the first thing in the morning, after returning from breakfast, and after returning from dinner. On each occasion he was required to deposit at the gate one of these tickets, which were afterwards sorted by the clerks, and entered in the time-book. In this way, if a man failed to come to his work, his ticket would be missing, and the time during which he was absent would not be entered; a corresponding amount being deducted from his week's wages.

On the Saturday, each man's time was made up from the book; and his wages calculated accordingly, and the amount entered against his name. The money due to each man was then counted out and placed in a small tin box, with a ticket, on which was written the man's name and number, and the amount of wages paid to him.

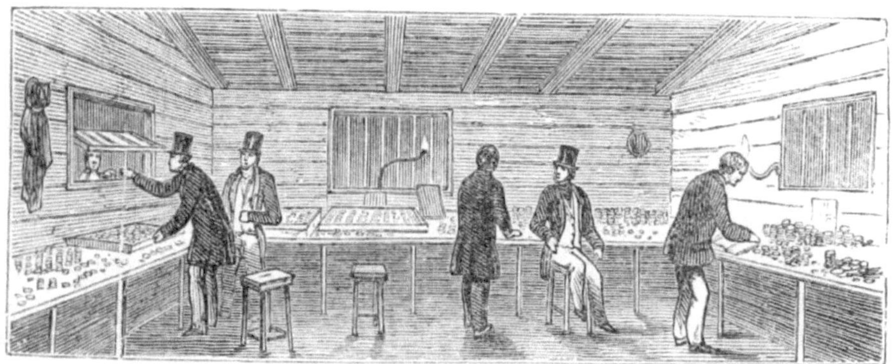

THE INTERIOR OF THE PAY-OFFICE.

All this was done in the time-keeper's office, which was conveniently placed near the entrance to the works. When all the preliminary arrangements had been completed, the workmen's bell was rung, and they assembled (a motley and sometimes clamorous crowd) round the pay-office, which was provided with two small openings through which the payments were made.

THE MEN TAKING THEIR WAGES AT THE PAY-OFFICE.

Two men stationed outside the office then called over the numbers of the workmen, who presented themselves, in the order in which they were called, at the pay-windows, where each man took the small box passed out to him with the money, and left the box in passing out at the gate. If any man considered the amount of wages paid to him not correct, he presented the ticket given to him with the wages at the office on the Monday morning following, when the matter was arranged by the time-keeper.

Any person acquainted with the irregular habits of vast numbers of our workmen, who will often be absent from their work a quarter of a day, and at other times a whole day, thus varying the amount of wages due at the end of the week to almost every man, will at once see that, without a well-arranged system, such as that described, the payment of so large a body of men would have occupied as many days as it really did hours. The engravings annexed, in illustration of this part of our subject, will convey to the reader some idea of the scene we have endeavoured to describe, though it must fall far short of the picturesque reality.

THE WORKMEN WAITING TO BE PAID.

GENERAL STATISTICS

T is with great pleasure that we are able to mention that, notwithstanding the difficult character of some of the work, and the extreme rapidity with which it was carried on, very few accidents of importance occurred; a circumstance which must be ascribed to the great care taken by the contractors for the safety of the men while engaged in their work: and in the cases where the accidents that occurred were of a serious or fatal kind, their origin was mostly to be traced to a neglect of those precautions which the men were constantly urged and ordered to take.

A few statistics of the quantities of different parts of the work not already mentioned will complete this portion of our subject. The whole amount of iron-work in the building is stated at about 4000 tons; and about 1,200 loads of timber were required for the wood-work. There are 2,941 trussed gutters in the roof, and 1,495 glazed sashes were required to inclose the sides of the building. As many as 316 iron girders were cast, in one week, and 442 lengths of the Paxton's gutters were cut out by the machinery in the same time. No less than 18,392 squares of glass, containing 62,508 feet superficial, or about one-and-a-half acres, were also fixed in one week.

It may be further mentioned that the weight of the different parts forming the flat ridge-and-furrow roofing amounts to three-and-a-quarter pounds per foot superficial, on the whole surface; the weight of the arched roof of the transept, including the ribs, amounts to five-and-three-quarter pounds per superficial foot; and the timbers and boards of the gallery floor weigh eight-and-a-half pounds to the superficial foot: from these data the actual weight on the different girders may be calculated.

The light iron-work, with the exception of some of the gallery railing, was cast at the works of the contractors near Birmingham; and the remainder, including the columns, girders, &c., was distributed between their own foundry, and those of the Messrs. Cochrane, of Wood Side, and Mr. Jobson, of Holly Hall, both near Dudley. The wrought-iron was supplied by Messrs. Fothergill, and the timber by Messrs. Dowson and Co.

THE PARTI-COLOURED PAINTING

HE coloured decoration introduced in finishing the painting of the building is a subject which has been much discussed, and many suggestions have been made by persons generally received as authorities on the subject. The system adopted was proposed by Mr. Owen Jones, under whose active superintendence it has been carried out. That gentleman explained his reasons for its adoption, and the effect which he expected it to produce, in a lecture at the Institute of British Architects, on the 16th of December, 1850, some portions of which are submitted to our readers:—

"It is not necessary for me to describe the building, the painting of which we are now about to discuss, as it is well known to most of you by its marvellous dimensions, the simplicity of its construction, and the advantage which has been taken of the power which the repetition of simple forms will give in producing grandeur of effect; and I wish now to show that this grandeur may be still further enhanced by a system of colouring which, by marking distinctly every line in the building, will increase the height, the length, and the bulk.

"The very nature of the material of which this building is mainly constructed, viz., iron, requires that it should be painted. On what principle shall we do this? Should we be justified in adopting a simple tint of white or stone colour, the usual method of painting iron? Now, it must be borne in mind that this building will be covered on the south side, and over the whole of the roof, with canvass, so that there can be but little light and shade. The myriads of similar lines, therefore, of which the building is composed, falling one before the other, would lose all distinctness, and form, in fact, one dull cloud overhanging the Exhibition.

"A line of columns (as it may be seen even now at the building) would present the effect of a white wall, and it would be impossible, in the distance, to distinguish one column from another. This mode of painting would have the further disadvantage of rendering the building totally unconnected with the various objects it is to contain.

"May the building be painted of a dark colour, like the roofs of some of our railway-stations? This, equally with the white method, would present one mass of indistinctness; the relief of the cast-iron would disappear, and each column and girder would present to the eye but a flat silhouette.

"Let us now consider the building as painted with some pale neutral tint, dull green or buff. In doing this we should be perfectly safe, as, provided the colours were not too pale so as to be indistinct, or too dark so as sensibly to affect the eye, we could hardly make a mistake. Yet how tame and monotonous would be the result! It would be necessary that this tint, whichever we might choose, should be of a very subdued neutral character, in order to avoid the difficulty well known to mounters of drawings and painters of picture-galleries, viz., that in proportion as you incline to any particular shade of colour, so in that exact proportion you injure or destroy those objects it is intended to relieve which may have similar colour. To this, then, we should be reduced — a dull monotonous colour without character. How unworthy this would be of the great occasion! How little would it impress the public! How little would it teach the artist! It would be to cut instead of patiently to unravel the knot.

"We are now brought to the consideration of the only other well-defined system which presents itself, namely, parti-colouring. This, I conceive, if successfully worked out, would bring the building and its contents into perfect harmony, and it would fitly carry out one of the objects for which this Exhibition was formed, namely, that of promoting the union of the fine-arts with manufactures. It would be an experiment on an immense scale, which, if successful, would tend to dispel the prejudices of those whose eyes are yet unformed to colour, to develope the imperfect appreciations of others, and to save this country from the reproach which foreign visitors, more educated in this particular than ourselves, would not fail to make were the building otherwise painted; it would everywhere bring out the construction of the building, which, as I said before, would also appear higher, longer, and more solid."

Mr. Jones then adduced the practice of the ancient and mediæval artists, and explained the kind of colours they generally adopted, mentioning that in the best periods of art the primary colours were chiefly or exclusively used.

"In the decoration of the Exhibition building I therefore propose to use the colours blue, red, and yellow, in such relative quantities as to neutralise or destroy each other; thus no one colour will be dominant or fatiguing to the eye, and all the objects exhibited will assist, and be assisted by, the colours of the building itself.

"In house-decoration we occasionally find a run on one colour; thus we have a green room, a pink room, and a red room; but it would obviously be unwise to adopt any one colour for this building, whose contents will be of all imaginable hues from white to black. Discarding, on the other hand, the perfect neutral white as unfit for the occasion, we naturally adopt the colours blue, red, and yellow, in or near the neutral proportions of eight, five, and three; but to avoid any harsh antagonism of the primary colours when in contact, or any undesired complementary secondaries arising from the immediate proximity of the primaries, I propose, in all cases, to interpose a line of white between them, which will soften them and give them their true value.

"As one of the objects of decorating a building is to increase the effect of light and shade, the best means of using blue, red, and yellow is to place blue, which retires, on the concave surfaces; yellow, which advances, on the convex; and red, the colour of the middle distance, on the horizontal planes; and the neutral white on the vertical planes.

"Following out this principle on the building in question, we have red for the under-side of the girders, yellow on the round portions of the columns, and blue in the hollow parts of the capitals.

"Now, it is necessary not only to put the several colours in the right places, but also to use them in their due proportions to each other.

"Mr. Field, in his admirable works on colour, has shown by direct experiment that white light consists of blue, red, and yellow, neutralising each other in the proportions of eight, five, and three. It will readily be seen, that the nearer we can arrive at this state of neutrality the more harmonious and light-giving will a building become; and an examination of the most perfect specimens of harmonious colouring of the ancients will show that this proportion has generally obtained among them; that is to say, broadly, there has been as much blue as the yellow and red put together, the light and the shade balancing each other.

"Of course, we cannot in decorating buildings always command the exact proportions of coloured surface which we require; but the balance of colours can always be obtained by a change in the colours themselves. Thus, if the surfaces to be coloured should give too much yellow, we should make the red more crimson and the blue more purple; that is, we should take the yellow out of them. So, if we had too much blue, we should make the yellow more orange, and the red more scarlet.

"A practised eye will as readily do this as a musician can tune a musical instrument; it is here that science abandons the artist, who must trust to his own perceptions, cultivated by renewed trials and repeated failures."

In concluding, Mr. Jones said, with reference to some specimens of the proposed decoration which had been executed, "I would ask you to banish from your minds the glare of light by which this decoration is now seen—to forget the rough foreground, where men are engaged in every variety of occupation for the completion of this great building; and I would ask you to fill it in imagination with the gorgeous products of every clime. I would ask you to picture to yourselves in the foreground the brilliant primaries, blue, red, and yellow—the rich secondaries, purple, amber, and green, moulded in forms of every conceivable diversity; and, lastly, against them the darker tertiaries fading into neutral perspective.

"The conception of such an effect, difficult even to the artist accustomed to abstract his attention from present interruptions and to calculate future harmonies, is impossible to the uninstructed spectator, who, from the experimental decoration of a single column, draws a premature and, necessarily, a fallacious inference as to the collective effect of the whole.

"From my brother architects I hope for a more patient, a more comprehensive, and a fairer appreciation; for myself, I have a confident hope, grounded on the experience of years devoted to this particular branch of art, that the principles and plans I have had the honour to propose to the Royal Commission, for the decoration of this magnificent structure, will be found, when complete, not to disappoint the public expectations, or to prove wholly unworthy of the great occasion."

In this lecture, Mr. Owen Jones asked his hearers, and the public generally, to suspend their final judgment upon his system of colouring until the whole should be completed, and the building filled with the objects to be exhibited, as he considered that many of the objections which were raised to his proposition resulted from a want of consideration of the ultimate effect to be produced by the whole, when completed and occupied; and so far as this effect has been realised, we believe it has inclined the public opinion more in favour of the coloured decoration than originally, when it was undoubtedly very strongly commented upon in various quarters. Without venturing to express any opinion ourselves, we may trust that Mr. Owen Jones's fondest hopes will be fully realised.

VIEW OF THE BUILDING FROM THE NORTH BANK OF THE SERPEN-TINE.

THE WATER SUPPLY

HE supply of water necessary both for the protection of this enormous building from fire, and for the use of fountains and machinery to be exhibited, is furnished at a very liberal rate by the Chelsea Waterworks' Company. It is brought into the building by a 9-inch main pipe, at about the centre of its length, branching out into three 6-inch pipes, which extend throughout the whole length of the building. Short pipes branch off from these, terminating in fire-cocks, placed at such distances that a circle of 120-feet radius from any one of them will touch a similar circle described round the adjacent ones; by which means the whole extent of the building may be brought under the action of hose attached to each of the fire-cocks. The water is supplied at a pressure equal to a column of about seventy feet, so as to work the fountains that will be exhibited, and to play efficiently from hose in case of any accident by fire. The quantity which the Company have undertaken to supply is 300,000 gallons a day.

THE STABILITY OF THE BUILDING

HE subject of the strength and stability of the building is one on which considerable anxiety has been felt, both by the public at large and by those professional bodies more capable of forming a correct judgment upon it. In the prolonged discussion which followed the reading of Mr. Wyatt's paper at the Institution of Civil Engineers, many points of objection were raised which seemed at first sight of a very serious nature; but, in most cases, the answers that were given to them were perfectly satisfactory. The two greatest difficulties raised were, firstly, the enormous surface presented by the exterior to the pressure of the wind, with apparently but a slight power of resistance; and, secondly, the construction of the galleries, which, it was thought, would not be able to resist the vibratory motion likely to be produced by great numbers of people walking upon them. The results of several calculations were adduced on the occasion alluded to in support of the objections on the first point; but perhaps the best answer that could be given to them was the circumstance mentioned by Mr. Fox—that on the 5th of that month (January) the pressure of the wind, which blew a perfect gale, was not only much above the average, but very nearly reached the greatest amount known within a considerable period in London—about 25lbs. per square foot; and that as the building, although in an incomplete state, had resisted that pressure without receiving any injury, it was fair to conclude that, when finished, it would be able to sustain the greatest force which the wind could be reasonably expected to exert upon it.

The question of the strength of the galleries was one of even greater importance than the other, as, in case of any failure in that part of the building, human life must almost inevitably have been sacrificed to a great extent. It was therefore deemed necessary to ascertain, as far as was practicable, by experiment, that their strength was abundantly sufficient; and in Mr. Wyatt's paper, as printed, the following description of the experiments instituted for this purpose will be found.

TESTING THE GALLERIES

N the interval between the reading of this paper and its going to press a series of experiments have been tried to ascertain the action of these galleries under the strain of a moving load. A complete bay, twenty-four feet square, was constructed, raised slightly from the ground, consisting of the four cast-iron girders, with the connecting-pieces at the angles, and on this the timbers and boards of the flooring. Rows of planks the full width of the platform led up to it and down from it, so that a body of men as wide as the gallery might be able to march up and down in close rank.

"The area of the platform was first covered over with labourers packed as closely together as possible; but no action of walking, running, or jumping that 300 men could perform did any injury whatever to it, and the greatest deflection of the girders did not exceed a quarter of an inch. Soldiers of the corps of Royal Sappers and Miners were then substituted for the contractors' men; and although the perfect regularity of their step in marking time sharply appeared a remarkably severe test, a minute examination of the construction after the completion of the experiments showed that no damage whatever had been done by their evolutions.

"But as the Commissioners were deeply impressed with the necessity of thoroughly convincing the public, who should visit the Exhibition, that they might feel perfectly secure in every part of the building, it was deemed desirable to apply a still further test to the actual galleries as they stand; as it might perhaps be said that the single bay which had been experimented upon was not similarly circumstanced to those forming parts of the building.

TESTING THE GALLERY FLOOR.

VIEW OF THE BOILER HOUSE.

"For this purpose a very ingenious apparatus was devised by the late Mr.

Field, President of the Institution of Civil Engineers, for testing the stability of the galleries *in situ*, and on being applied over the greater part of the building not a single bolt or girder gave way under its action. This apparatus consisted of eight square wooden frames divided into thirty-six compartments, each just capable of containing and allowing to rotate a 68-pounder shot. The surfaces of the balls placed in each of these compartments came in contact with the gallery floor, the frames themselves being attached to one another and running along the floor by means of castors fixed at the angles; the whole apparatus being drawn along by a number of men. Two hundred and eighty-eight 68-pound shot confined in a limited area were thus set rolling over more than half the extent of the galleries; when, not the slightest mishap having occurred, the experiment was considered decisive, and a persistence in it deemed unnecessary."

The pressure obtained in this experiment amounted to about a hundred pounds per square foot, and it had been ascertained that the greatest pressure caused by packing men together as closely as possible was equal to about ninety-five pounds per square foot; so that the testing force applied was considered amply sufficient, as a considerable portion of the surface of the gallery will be occupied by light articles exhibited in the cases and stalls which are placed along the centre of the gallery, where a great weight would have most effect.

This ingenious method of proving the strength of the galleries *in situ*, without endangering those engaged in the experiment, is admirable; and the result of the proof will no doubt allay all fear in the mind of the public as to the safety of this portion of the building.

GENERAL ADVANTAGES OF THE BUILDING

T is always much easier to point out the defects of any work than its ex-cellences; whilst we may, therefore, safely leave the former, as regards our present subject, to be discovered and enlarged upon by those who may be perhaps more competent than ourselves, we will attempt to point out what we conceive to be some of the advantages obtained in the present building.

One of the principal of these, considering throughout the purpose of the structure, is, perhaps, the uninterrupted view of the interior which the spectator may obtain from any point of the building—a matter of great importance to the general grandeur of its effect. From the galleries more particularly, which will be less obstructed by large objects, the eye of the spectator will be able to range from end to end of the vast edifice; while the transparency of the material used for the roof allows every object to be brilliantly illuminated. The slender lines of the supports, though they serve to sustain a protecting covering, scarcely interrupt the view of the objects protected, and the absence of any fixed divisions or partitions enables all the articles exhibited to be so arranged as to suit the peculiar requirements of each particular class; while the ample space between the supports has admitted of the formation of large open avenues for the free passage of visitors, who may thus reach as readily the remotest corners of the building as those situated near the entrances; and whenever the visitor may find himself fatigued by the labour of sight-seeing, he will be sure to find himself near one of the numerous exit-doors, whereby he may immediately free himself from the crowd of spectators.

From the simplicity of the details of the construction, and their constant recurrence, it will be seen that so long as the ends of the building were left incomplete, its size could easily be limited or expanded, so as to include that precise amount of space which, up to the last moment when the point could be kept open, appeared most likely to be required. This simplicity of arrangement will also be found very advantageous in case the building is removed after the termination of its present temporary purpose; as the parts may be easily separated without much injury, and as readily re-erected, either as a whole, or even in many separate buildings, having the same arrangement of parts, without the same general form or appearance.

It has been calculated that the passages remaining in the building, after deducting the space appropriated to the objects exhibited, will hold more than 100,000 persons; though it is not to be expected that half that number will be collected there at one time. The ventilation and supply of fresh air for so vast a throng was therefore a matter of the first importance; and the means already described for accomplishing this great object are so ample, that any inconvenience from oppressive heat or foul air can hardly be expected. The canvass with which the roof is covered will not only serve to modify the heat of the sun in the interior, but it is expected that if it be watered by the hose of engines, it may even reduce the temperature within to considerably below that of the external air. From his experience in glass-houses for horticultural purposes, Mr. Paxton speaks confidently on this point.

The arrangement of the construction of the building resting on isolated instead of continuous supports, will enable all traces of it to be readily effaced from the site if it is removed; and, on the other hand, if it remains, it is evidently peculiarly suited to form a vast winter-garden and public promenade.

CONCLUSION

EFORE taking leave of the reader who may have patiently followed us thus far, a few words may be necessary on the general arrangement of the articles to be exhibited in the building whose outline and details we have been endeavouring to trace. The first classification is geographical. All the western half of the building is given to England, and the eastern, which is rather the larger of the two, to foreign countries; the space assigned to each country being distinctly defined, so as to avoid the possibility of any disputes. As far as it was possible, the space for each country is so arranged as to have a frontage towards the main central avenue, and in most cases occupies a strip the whole width of the building; the visitor, therefore, passing up and down the length, will not miss out any country.

In the central avenue, and immediately on either side of it, are placed the most remarkable specimens of objects coming under the class of fine-arts, or otherwise sufficiently remarkable to entitle them to such a prominent place. Behind these, in the side avenues, will be found the various specimens of manufactured articles; and along the outside longitudinal avenues are placed, on the south side, those belonging to the class of raw products (a portion being devoted to agricultural implements), and the projecting portion of the building on the north side forms the hall of machinery, which is separated by a partition of glazed sashes from the rest of the building. Many of the articles will be grouped in courts, an arrangement which the construction particularly leads to; and these will probably form some of the greatest attractions in the Exhibition, each being, as it were, complete in itself, and the inclosures preventing the eye from being distracted by distant objects. To enter further into the detail of this part of the subject would be foreign to the purpose of this work, the building itself being our text.

We have now, we believe, completed the pleasant task we proposed to ourselves at the outset, and we hope that in doing so we may have been able to render interesting to our general readers this description of operations, usually occupying the attention of the technical professions only. With this intention, we have avoided as far as possible the use of technical terms, which would be a dead letter to the uninitiated, at the risk, perhaps, of being considered inaccurate by those acquainted with all the details of the subject.

So many men whose eminent talent is well known and appreciated by the public have been engaged in perfecting the designs and carrying out the erection of this vast structure, that the critic should be one of no mean reputation who would venture to raise even a small voice of individual criticism on its merits. We have considered it, therefore, to be our part rather to record the opinions of others on any points where a discussion has been raised than to trouble the reader with any personal views, which would, perhaps, have only appeared impertinent.

The nature and extent of the difficulties which have been successfully surmounted in carrying out this great work can only be fully appreciated by those intimately acquainted with all its structural details and with its rapid progress; and its completion in so short a period must be regarded as a striking instance of the productive power and spirit of commercial enterprise of this country, while the fact of its being defrayed by the voluntary contributions of the people will illustrate in an interesting manner to our continental visitors that principle of self-government which forms the basis of all our institutions, and the spirit of private enterprise which characterises most of our great undertakings.

The illustrative engravings with which we have endeavoured to render more interesting the descriptive details, necessarily somewhat dry to the general reader, are only intended to convey general ideas, without attempting that minute accuracy which would be required in a more technical work; and with reference to some of them we take this opportunity of acknowledging the assistance our artists have derived from views already published elsewhere, others having been exclusively drawn for the present work.

We have much pleasure in presenting our readers, in the Appendix, with views and descriptions of two of the most striking designs sent in the first competition for the building, the materials for which have been kindly afforded us by their respective authors; and we may remind the reader that these two designs were specially mentioned by the Building Committee in their Report already quoted. In the same place some interesting documents connected with the building will also be found, which we were unable to insert in the text.

VIEW OF SOUTH FRONT OF THE BUILDING.

APPENDIX.

LIST OF COMPETITORS FOR THE BUILDING PROPOSED TO BE ERECTED IN HYDE PARK.

Mons. Acollas, Architecte, 33, Rue Lafayette, à Paris.

Messrs. Aickin and Capes, 1, Clarence-street, Islington.

W. Albon, Esq., 32, Abingdon-street, Westminster.

C. B. Allen, Architect, 9, Great College-street, Westminster.

F. C. Anderson, Esq., 9, Holles-street, Cavendish-square.

Architekton (W. Bardwell, 4, Great Queen-street, Westminster).

Henry Ashton, Esq., 50A, Lower Brooke-street.

John S. Austin, Architect, Bedford.

William Austin, Esq., High-street, East Dereham, Norfolk.

C. Badger, Esq., Architect, 40, Rue Blanche, Paris.

R. Baly, Esq., 14, Buckingham-street, Adelphi.

Alfred Beaumont, Architect, 5, Warwick Chambers, Beak-street.

Richard Bell, Architect, Pope's Head Chambers, Cornhill.

W. Bell, Esq., Clift Cottage, Coronation-road, Bristol.

Thomas Bellamy, Esq., 8, Charlotte-street, Bedford-square.

Mons. Felix Belleflamme, Brussels.

J. S. Benest, Esq., 21, Rutland-street, Hampstead-road.

J. H. Bertram, M. Inst. C. E., Reading.

John Black, Esq., 33, Ernest-street, Regent's Park.

E. Blatchley, Esq., Jun., 362, Oxford-street.

Mons. Alphonse Botrel, Architecte, 121, Rue Poissonnière, Paris.

A. W. Boulnois, Esq., Bazaar, King-street, Baker-street.

W. Boyle, Esq., 5, Little George-street, Westminster.

R. Brandon, Architect, 11, Beaufort-buildings, Strand.

R. Broad, Esq., Horseley Works, Tipton.

B. Broadbridge, Architect, 35, Ladbroke-square, Notting-hill.

F. Brown, Esq., Francis-street, Torrington-square.

R. Brown, Esq., 41, Lord-street, Liverpool.

J. B. Bunning, Esq., Guildhall.

George A. Burn, Architect, George-place, Hammersmith.

H. P. Burt, Esq., 238, Blackfriars-road.

John G. Grace, Esq., 14, Wigmore-street.

E. I. C., Alnwick.

Mons. J. Cailloux, 25, Marché St. Honoré, Paris.

A. F. Campbell, Esq., 104, Pall Mall, Reform Club.

Henry Case, Esq., 19, Hanover Villas, Kensington Park.

James Catt, Esq., Blackheath Park.

Mons. J. Charpentier, Architecte, 15, Rue Larochefoucalt, Paris.

J. Claringbull, Esq., 95, Herbert-street, New North-road.

Mons. Henri van Cléemputte, Laon, France.

Mons. J. P. Cluysenaar, Architecte, Bruxèlles.

J. Colshurst, Esq., 36, Jermyn-street, St. James's.

John Colson, Architect, Winchester.

Mons. J. W. Conrad, Chief Engineer, La Haye, Holland.

C. E. Coote, Esq., Clifton.

W. R. Corson, Architect, 3, Albion-place, Leeds.

H. Courtney, Esq., 39, Awylne-road, Canonbury-square, Islington.

David Cowan, Esq., 9, Hungerford-street, Strand.

Mons. Crémont, 10, Place des Vosges, Paris.

W. Cruikshank, Esq., 24, Duke-street.

Mons. E. Damas de Culture, 20, Rue Mazayran, Paris.

G. J. Darley, Esq., C.E., 7, Kildare-street, Dublin.

Mons. A. Delaage, 6, Place de l'Oratoire du Louvre, Paris.

W. Dennis, Esq., Church-street, Hackney.

Charles Downes, Esq., 29, Coleshill-street, Eaton-square.

Francis Drake, Esq., 11, Calthorpe-street, Gray's-inn-road.

Henry Duesbury, Architect, Kensington Gore.

Mons. Duflocq, 96, Rue Rochechouart, Paris.

Mons. Dupuy, 9, Rue Duplessés, Versailles.

Mons. Dusillion, Architecte, Thoune Suisse, Faubourg St. Germain, Paris.

Mons. A. Durand, Moulins, France.

O. C. Edwards, Esq., Gloucester.

J. Eldudge, Esq., 16, Somerset-place, New Road, Commercial-rd. East.

J. Elliott, Architect, 28, Portland-terrace, Southampton.

M. G. Fétar van Elven, Architecte, Amsterdam.

D. Erskine, Esq., 58, Clerk-street, Edinburgh.

W. J. Everitt, Esq., 1, Garden-street, Stepney-green.

Mons. Théodore Faure, 2, Little Argyle-street, Regent-street.

Mons. F. Desaint Félix, and E. E. White, Architects, Ipswich.

Mons. Henri Fevre, Architecte, 41, Rue de Vaugirard, à Paris.

F. Finlay, Esq., 26, Duke-street, Westminster.

Charles Folkard, Esq., C.E., 56, King-street, Whitehall.

David Colin Forbes, Esq., Stirling.

James Forrest, Esq., C.E., 25, Great George-street.

W. Freebody, Esq., 9, Duke-street, Westminster.

S. C. Fripp, Architect, Bristol.

L. Fürges, Architecte, Crefeld.

C. E. G., Warwick.

A. Garrard. Esq., Surveyor.

Mons. Gaulle, 81, Rue Française, à Calais.

Arthur Gearing, Esq., 2, Ranelagh-street, Leamington Spa.

William Geggie, Esq., Knaresbro'.

J. Gibson, Esq., Great Western Railway, Paddington.

Robert Gilingham, Esq., 31, Clarence-road, Kentish Town.

Mons. Godebœuf, Architecte, 12, Place Breda, à Paris.

C. W. Gooch, Esq., 42, Connaught-terrace, Edgeware-road.

John Gould, Esq., Tottenham Park, Wiltshire.

Richard Greene, Esq., F.S.A., Sec. to Lichfield Architectural Society.

Edmund W. Grubb, Esq., Newnham, Gloucestershire.

Robert S. Grubb, Esq., Newham-on-Severn, Gloucestershire.

T. R. Guppy, Esq., Naples.

J. C. Haddan, Esq., 29, Bloomsbury-square.

Thomas Roberts Hannaford, Architect, 21, Trigon-terrace, Kennington.

O. Hansard, Architect, 2, Kensington-gardens-terrace, Hyde Park.

Robert Hardy, Carpenter, 32, North Conduit-street, Bethnal-green.

John Thornhill Harrison, Esq., East Bolden, near Gateshead.

J. P. Harrison, Esq., 11, Chancery-lane.

Thomas Haw, Esq., 27, Prospect-terrace, Globe-road, Mile-end.

Thomas Hayes, Esq., 7, St. George's-terrace, Hyde Park.

Samuel Heilton, Esq., 54, Red Cross-street, City.

Mons. J. Henard, 98, Rue St. Lazarre, Paris.

James Hendrey, Esq., 4, Pancras-lane, Cheapside.

J. Hewitt, Esq., Oxford.

W. S. Hollands, Esq., 37, King William-street.

Mons. Hector Horeau, 70, Rue Richelieu, Paris.

George Horton, Esq., 6, Green-street, Grosvenor-square.

Albert P. Howell, Architect, 2, Holywell-street, Westminster.

Mons. C. Huchon, 28, Rue Meslay, Paris.

Benjamin Hurwitz, Esq., 1, Brydges-street, Strand.

John Imray, Esq., Engineer, 12, Howley-street, Lambeth.

A. Jackson, Esq., Barkhart House, Orpington, Kent.

Mons. Ch. Schœch Jaquet, 238, Rue de la Vertasse, Geneva.

Charles Jayne, Architect, 7, Chancery-lane.

Adam Jizkowski, Architect to the Government, Warsaw.

Joseph Jopling, Esq., Felton Villa, Finchley-road.

H. J. Kaye, Esq., 63, Sloane-street, Knightsbridge.

G. P. Kennedy and R. Kennedy, Esqrs., Sussex Chambers, Duke-street, St. James's.

J. T. Knowles, Esq., 1, Raymond-buildings, Gray's Inn.

Herr Friedrich Krahe, Brunswick.

Louis Kûhne, Brunswick.

A Lady with great diffidence submits this plan.

M. Laves, Architect to the King of Hanover, Hanover.

Mons. A. G. Ledrut, Claremont.

S. W. Leonard, Assistant-Curator Micrological Society, 11, Upper Stamford-street, Waterloo-road.

W. B. Lewis, Esq., Rainbow-hill, Worcester.

R. Lobb, Esq., 8, Goulden-terrace, Barnsbury-road, Islington.

Locke Brothers, New Peckham.

Henry Lockwood, F.S.A., and William Mawson, Architects, Bradford.

Henry Lote, Esq., 51, Brompton-row.

R. Lovely, Esq., C.E., 1, Victoria-terrace, Queen's-road, Nottingham.

George Mackenzie, Esq., 3, Claremont-row, Barnsbury-road, Islington.

Messrs. Magni and Thummeloup, 26, Boulevard du Temple, Paris.

R. Mallet, Esq., Victoria Foundry, Dublin.

Mansell and Elliott, Architects, Halkin-street West, Belgrave-square.

R. M. Marchant, Esq., 18, Great George-street.

P. J. Margary, Esq., Dawlish, Devonshire.

W. P. Marshall, Esq., Temple-buildings, New-street, Birmingham.

D. Mickle, Esq., 37, Queen-square, Bloomsbury.

Joseph Mitchell, Architect, St. James's-street, Sheffield.

J. Montheath, Esq., 10, Stanley-street, Paddington.

James Moon, Architect, 1, Millman-street, Bedford-row.

Captain W. S. Moorsom, 17½, Great George-street.

G. Morgan, Architect, 6, Charles-street, Westminster.

J. H. Muller, Gaes, Holland.

Charles C. Nelson, Esq., 30, Hyde-park-gardens, London.

Mons. C. Frédéric Nepveu, 13, Place d'Armes, Versailles.

W. Nethersole, Esq., C.E., 73, Oakley-square, St. Pancras.

I. W. Newberry, Esq., Hook Norton, Chipping Norton, Oxon.

Francis B. Newman, Architect, 14, Heathcote-street, Mecklenburgh-sq.

C. H. Newton, Esq., 92, Camden-road Villas, Regent's Park.

Mons. Paliard, 23, Rue d'Enghein, Paris.

E. Paraire, Architect, 16, Woodstock-street, Bond-street.

Mons. Henri le Pâtre, 47, Grande Rue de la Chapelle, St. Denis, Paris.

Thomas Peacock, Esq., High-street, Kensington.

J. D. Pemberton, Esq., Royal Agricultural College, Cirencester.

G. Perry, Architect, 42, Newington-place, Kennington.

Mons. Casimir Pétiaux, Paris.

William Radley, Chemical Engineer, Regent-street, Lambeth.

W. Railton, Esq., 12, Regent-street.

W. Rankin, Esq., Stirling.

W. Reed, Esq., Cannon Cottage Hill, Southampton.

Messrs. Reid and Butcher, Architects and Surveyors, 38, Red Lion-square, London.

Stanley Reilly, Architect, 3, Upper Kennington-green, Kennington.

George Banks Rennie, Esq., Whitehall-place.

Harry Ralph Ricardo, Esq., Beaulieu Lodge, Norwood, Surrey.

W. Riddle, Esq., East Temple Chambers, Whitefriars, Fleet-street.

H. S. Ridley, Architect, 31, Vincent-square, Westminster.

J. B. Roberts, Architect, Sleaford, Lincolnshire.

R. Roberta, Esq., Globe Works, Manchester.

Andrew John Robertson, Esq., C.E., Newcastle-upon-Tyne.

William Robertson, Esq., 12, Gordon-street, City-road.

A. Rosengarten, Architect, Hamburg.

Alex. M. Ross, Esq., 3, Parliament-street, Westminster.

Rough Draught, 42, Stainford-street.

Henry Rouse, Esq.

H. H. Russell, Esq., C.E., M.R.S.A.

W. Russell, Esq., 3, Frederick-street, Hampstead-road.

E. Ryde, Esq., 14, Upper Belgrave-place, Eaton-square.

George Sanderson, Esq., 136, Solly-street, Sheffield.

Charles Sanderson, Esq., Friar-street, Reading.

Robert Sandeman, Architect, Greenside, Edinburgh.

H. Savage, Esq., 22, Beaumont-street. Mary-le-bone.

W. Scurry, Esq., 7, Denbigh-place, Pimlico.

Sed quis custodiet Custodes.

J. P. Seddon, Esq., Gray's-inn-road.

J. R. Sewell, Esq., Carrington, near Nottingham.

Mons. A. Slater, Architecte, Elève de Mons. l'Architecte Cluysenaar.

E. Smallwood, Architect, 86, Park-street, Camden Town.

F. Smallman Smith, Esq., 18, Brunswick-st., Barnsbury-road, Islington.

C. H. Smith, Esq., 29, Clipstone-street.

J. M. Smith, Esq., 1, Chapel-place, Duke-street, Westminster.

W. J. Smith, Esq., 18, Bond-street, Commercial-road, Lambeth.

G. Campbell Smith, Esq., Banff.

Messrs. Soyer and Warrener, Reform Club.

Paul Sprenger, Esq., Architect to the Government, Vienna.

Herr Friederich Stammann, Hamburg.

Francis Sternitz, Esq., 10, Berner-street, Commercial-road East.

W. Stewart, Esq., Seacombe, Cheshire.

M. J. Stutely, Architect, 4, Doughty-street, Mecklenburgh-square.

H. Suckling, Esq., 1, Conduit-street, Regent-street.

George Tate, Esq., Bawtry, Yorkshire.

J. Taylor, Architect, 22, Parliament-street.

T. Taylor, Architect, 33, Clarendon-street, Oakley-square.

J. H. Taunton, Esq., 2, Gordon-place, Kensington.

D. W. Thomas, Esq., 20, St. Petersburg-place, Bayswater.

R. M. Thompson, Esq., 46, Leicester-square.

P. Thompson, Architect, 1, Osnaburgh-place, New-road.

F. Thompson, Esq., 15, Trafalgar-square, Peckham.

James Thrupp, Architect, 2, Park-place, Bath.

H. W. Todd and W. Allingham, 91, Newman-street, Oxford-street.

Richard Turner and Thomas Turner, Hammersmith Works, Dublin.

Henry Turner, Esq., Low Heaton, Haugh, Newcastle-on-Tyne.

F. Tyerman, Jun., Architect, 14, Parliament-street.

Mons. Véron, 2, Quai des Armes, Paris.

John Walker, Esq., Crooked-lane Chambers, King William-street.

George Wallis, Artist, and Henry Summers, Architect, 14, College-place, Camden Town.

J. N. Warren, Esq., C.E., 18, Adam-street, Adelphi.

J. E. Watson, Esq., 74, Grey-street, Newcastle-on-Tyne.

Henry Whitcombe, Esq., Slough.

George Wightwick, Architect, 3, Athenæum-terrace, Plymouth.

George Wilkie, Esq., C.E., 8, Powell-street West, King's-square.

George Wilkinson, Esq., Horsham.

S. J. Wilkinson, Esq., 7, Jeffry's-square, St. Mary Axe.

James Williams, Esq., 18, Westgate-buildings, Bath.

George Wilson, Esq., Knaresbro', Yorkshire.

Ralph Wilson, Architect, 16, Bridge-street, Westminster.

James G. Wilson, Esq., 18, Great George-street, Westminster,

Richard Winder, Esq., Fenchurch-street.

R. A. Withall, Architect, 80, Cheapside.

W. H. Wontner, Architect, St. Ann's-road, North Brixton.

Frederick Wood, Esq., 6, Franklin-road, Queen's-road, East Chelsea.

Thomas Worthington, Architect, 54, King-street, Manchester.

James Wylson, Architect, 112, Fyfe-place, Glasgow.

LIST A. ENTITLED TO FAVOURABLE AND HONOURABLE MENTION.

C. B. Allen, Architect, Great College-street, Westminster.

W. Allingham (and Todd), 91, Newman-street, Oxford-street.

Architekton (W. Bardwell, 4, Great Queen-street, Westminster).

H. Ashton, 50A, Lower Brooke-street.

C. Badger, Architect, Rue Blanche, Paris.

B. P. Baly (four designs).

R. Bell, Architect, Pope's Head Chambers, Cornhill.

Thomas Bellamy, Architect, Charlotte-street, Bedford-square.

J. H. Bertram, C. E., Reading.

A. Botrel, Architect, 121, Rue Poissonnière, Paris.

R. Brandon, Architect, Little Beaufort-buildings, Strand.

F. Brown, Francis-street, Torrington-square.

J. B. Bunning, Architect, Guildhall, City of London.

G. A. Burn, Architect, George-place, Hammersmith.

J. Cailloux, Architect, 25, Marché St. Honoré, Paris.

H. Case, 19, Hanover Villas, Kensington Park.

J. Charpentier, Architect, 15, Rue Larochefoucalt, Paris.

Henri Van Cléemputte, Architect, Laon, France.

J. P. Cluysenaar, Architect of King of the Belgians, Brussels.

J. W. Conrad, Chief Engineer, La Haye, Holland.

H. Courtney, Esq., 39, Alwyne-road, Canonbury-square, Islington.

Mons. Crémont, Architect, 10, Place des Vosges, Paris.

W. Cruikshank, 24, Duke-street.

A. Delaage, Architect, 6, Place de l'Oratoire du Louvre, Paris.

C. Downes, Coleshill-street, Eaton-square.

A. Durand, Moulins, France.

Mons. Dusillion, Architect, Thoune Suisse, Faubourg St. Germain, Paris.

M. G. Fétar Van Elven, Architect, Amsterdam.

H. Fevre, Architect, 41, Rue de Vaugirard, à Paris.

S. C. Fripp, Architect, Bristol.

Mons. Gaulle, 81, Rue Française, Calais.

A. Gearing, 2, Ranelagh-street, Leamington Spa.

Eugene Godebœuf, 12, Place Breda, Paris.

J. T. Harrison, East Bolden, near Gateshead.

T. Hayes, 7, St. George's-terrace, Hyde-park.

J. Henard, Architect, 98, Rue St. Lazarre, Paris.

H. Horeau, 70, Rue Richelieu, Paris.

C. Huchon, 28, Rue Meslay, Paris.

J. Imray, C. E., Howley-street, Lambeth.

Ch. Schœch Jaquet, 238, Rue de la Vertasse, Geneva.

Louis Kûhne, Brunswick.

J. T. Knowles, Architect, 1, Raymond-buildings, Gray's Inn.

M. Laves, Architect of the King, Hanover.

A. G. Ledrut, Clermont, France.

W. B. Lewis, Rainbow-hill, Worcester.

C. C. Nelson, 30, Hyde-park-gardens, London.

C. F. Nepveu, 13, Place d'Armes, Versailles.

Mons. Paliard, Rue d'Enghein, Paris.

H. le Pâtre, Architect, 47, Grande Rue de la Chapelle, St. Denis, Paris.

Casimir Pétiaux, Paris.

H. S. Ridley, Architect, 31, Vincent-square, Westminster.

J. B. Roberts, Architect, Sleaford, Lincolnshire.

A. Rosengarten, Architect, Hamburg.

H. Rouse, Esq.

W. Russell, 3, Frederick-street, Hampstead-road.

H. Savage, 22, Beaumont-street, Marylebone.

J. P. Seddon, Esq., Gray's-inn-road.

A. Slater, Architect, Elève de Mons. Cluysenaar.

F. Smallman Smith, 18, Brunswick-street, Barnsbury-road, Islington.

C. H. Smith, Clipstone-street, London.

Paul Sprenger, Architect, Vienna.

H. Sumners, Architect, 14, College-place, Camden Town.

Richard and Thomas Turner, Hammersmith Works, Dublin.

F. Tyerman, Jun., Architect, 14, Parliament-street.

Mons. Véron, 2, Quai des Ormes, Paris.

J. Watson, 74, Grey-street, Newcastle-upon-Tyne.

W. H. Wontner, Architect, St. Ann's-road, North Brixton.

T. Worthington, Architect, King-street, Manchester.

LIST B. ENTITLED TO FURTHER HIGHER HONORARY DIS-TINCTION.

C. Badger, Architect, Rue Blanche, Paris.

Thomas Bellamy, Architect, Charlotte-street, Bedford-square.

J. H. Bertram, C. E., Reading.

A. Botrel, Architect, 121, Rue Poissonnière, Paris.

J. Cailloux, Architect, 25, Marché St. Honoré, Paris.

Henri Van Cléemputte, Architect, Laon, France.

Mons. Crémont, Architect, 10, Place des Vosges, Paris.

A. Delaage, Architect, 6, Place de l'Oratoire du Louvre, Paris.

M. G. Fétar Van Elven, Architect, Amsterdam.

J. Henard, Architect, 98, Rue St. Lazarre, Paris.

H. Horeau, 70, Rue Richelieu, Paris.

C. Huchon, 28, Rue Meslay, Paris.

A. G. Ledrut, Clermont, France.

H. le Pâtre, Architect, 4K, Grande Rue de la Chapelle, St. Denis, Paris.

Casimir Pétiaux, Paris.

Paul Sprenger, Architect, Vienna.

Richard and Thomas Turner, Hammersmith Works, Dublin.

Mons. Véron, 2, Quai des Ormes, Paris.

EXTERIOR VIEW OF MONS. HOREAU'S DESIGN FOR THE BUILDING.

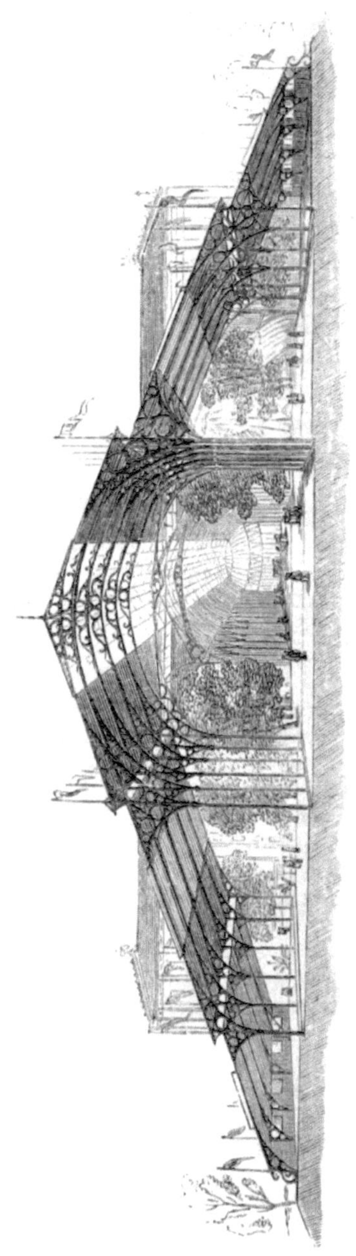

VIEW OF THE INTERIOR.

TWO OF THE COMPETITION DESIGNS.

The following descriptions and plates of two of the designs sent in competition for the Building, and specially mentioned by the Committee in their Report, are given from information obligingly furnished to us by their respective authors.

DESIGN BY M. HECTOR HOREAU, ARCHITECT, OF PARIS.

This was one of the most striking of all that were submitted to the Commission; it formed one immense hall, or shed, more than 2000 feet long, by about 270 feet wide throughout, with several small detached buildings on the north side, for refreshments, &c.

The interior of the main building was divided into five avenues, the centre one about ninety feet wide, those next adjoining rather more than fifty feet, and the outside ones about forty feet wide. Iron columns, about twenty-three feet apart, formed these avenues and supported arched ribs for the roof. One end of the building was semicircular, the other forming an ornamental façade, and about the centre of the length a transept was formed.

M. Horeau says: "Simplicity, grandeur, ready means of construction, and of increasing or diminishing the accommodation, and of removal if required, forming altogether a specimen of the most recent improvements introduced into the art of building—these are the principal objects which it has been sought to attain. The whole of the construction is of iron, without a single piece of wood, the foundation being executed in brick; the façade to be in metal, porcelain, and glass, the floor of asphalte, the roof to be principally covered with ornamental thick glass, in large dimensions, or ground glass with patterns.

"Of the trusses or arched ribs supporting the roof there were to be but three varieties, each in three pieces, with which the whole of the building could be erected. This subdivision of the roof-trusses would have facilitated the conversion of the building for other purposes; for, taken singly, or in various combinations, they would have formed many kinds of buildings for ordinary purposes. The attached buildings placed on the north side would have shown several modes of effecting this. The ornamental spandrils of the roof-trusses would be formed in stamped-work out of copper, and gilt.

"The façade shows at a glance the purpose of the building, as well as its interior disposition, in which the different widths of avenues would afford space for objects of all varieties of dimensions. The façade itself was to be formed with tracery or trellis-work of cast-iron, the lower part being covered with sheet-iron; the cornice and ornamental panels of porcelain; the medallions in coloured stone-ware; the doors and inclosures of metal, silvered and gilt; the ornamental details to be either cast or stamped; the scrolls in the panels being in coloured glass or mosaic.

"The pediment is crowned with a group of figures representing the Genius of Industry crowning the Arts and Sciences; in the cornice are placed the names of all the principal cities of the world, and the names of eminent men in panels. In the medallions are represented allegorical figures of the different branches of science and industry. At the angles of the building are placed trophies, the base of which would serve as guard-houses."

The engravings will serve to show the general effect of this design in its interior and exterior.

DESIGN BY MESSRS. R. AND T. TURNER, OF DUBLIN.

In this design also the interior was arranged as one uninterrupted space, about 1,940 feet long, and 408 wide, the roof in one span rising about 120 feet above the floor; the supports, consisting of semicircular ribs, forming the interior into three avenues, the centre one 200 feet wide and the full height, the side ones 104 feet wide and about sixty feet high. In the centre of the length a transept was proposed, and the square area at the meeting of that with the central avenue was to be covered with a glass dome.

The ends of the building, as well as those of the transept, were to be filled in with tracery in the upper part, a colonnade below protecting the entrances. Galleries, if necessary, were to be placed in the side avenues. The construction of this building was proposed to be principally of wrought iron, which would have given to the circular ribs and other parts a great lightness of effect; but, on the other hand, the difficulties of producing and putting together such an enormous amount of wrought-iron work in so short a space of time as that required was considered an almost insuperable objection to the design. Large portions of the roof were to be covered with glass, so as to admit an abundance of light into the interior.

The accompanying views of the exterior and interior of this design, from the simplicity of the arrangement, consisting of a repetition of similar parts, require but little description for their elucidation.

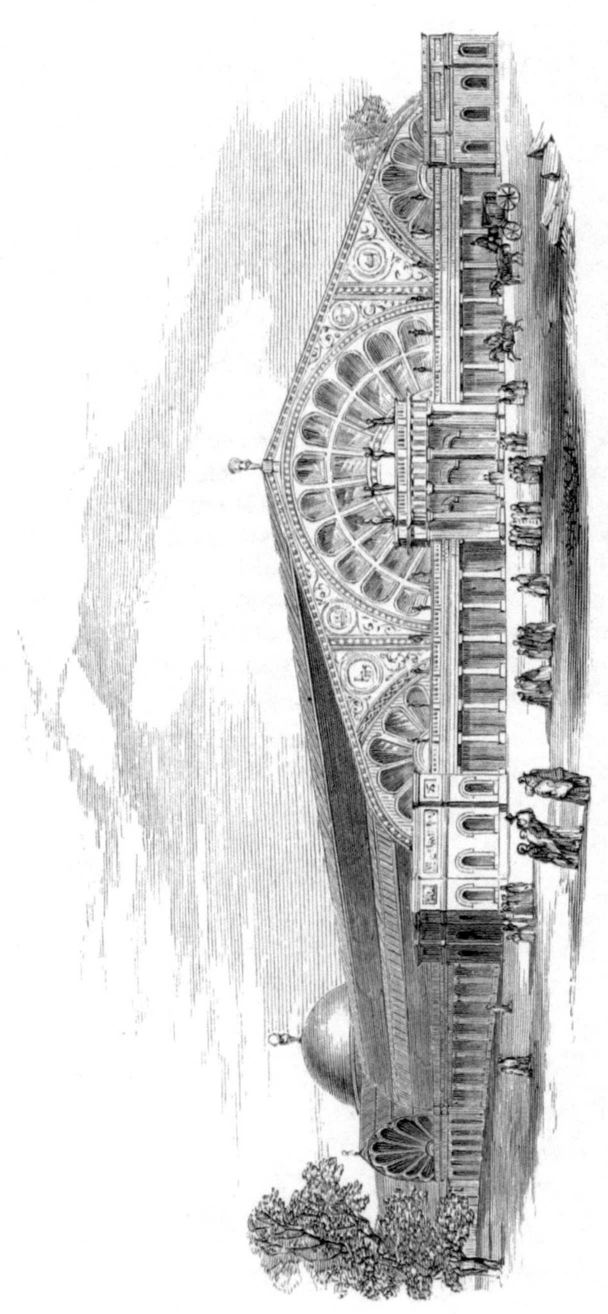

VIEW OF EXTERIOR FROM ONE END OF MESSRS. TURNERS' DESIGN
FOR THE BUILDING.

TRANSVERSE SECTION, AND VIEW OF THE INTERIOR OF MESSRS. R. AND T. TURNER'S DESIGN.

MEMORANDUM ON THE SITE.

Return to an Order of the Honourable the House of Commons, dated 1st July, 1850;
for

COPY of a Letter addressed by the Commissioners of the Exhibition of 1851 to the Lords of the Treasury, inclosing Memorandum as to the Site of the Exhibition Building in Hyde Park.

Palace of Westminster, 1st July, 1850.

Sir,—I am directed by her Majesty's Commissioners for the Exhibition of 1851 to transmit to you herewith, for the information of the Lords Commissioners of her Majesty's Treasury, a memorandum of the grounds on which the present site has been selected for the Exhibition, and of the proceedings that have been taken in consequence of that selection.—I have, &c.

(Signed) Stafford H. Northcote.

The Right Honourable W. G. Hayter, M.P., &c. &c. &c.

Memorandum of the grounds on which the site has been selected for the Exhibition of 1851, and of the proceedings which have been taken in consequence of that selection, prepared for the information of the Lords of the Treasury by the Royal Commissioners for promoting the Exhibition.

1. It is within the knowledge of the Lords of the Treasury, that from the time of the earliest announcement of the proposed Exhibition it has always been intended that it should take place in the Metropolis. Not only was such an intention matter of notoriety at the time that the question of issuing a Royal Commission was under consideration, but the Commission itself, when issued formally recited that it was proposed "To establish an Enlarged Exhibition of the Works of Industry of all Nations, to be holden in London, in the year 1851;" and it was to further the holding of such an exhibition that the present Commissioners were specially appointed.

2. Considering the importance of the undertaking, and the circumstances attending its promulgation, the selection of the Metropolis as its intended locality appears to have been both natural and proper. It will be borne in mind that the exhibitions which have from time to time been held in foreign countries have generally, and, as the Commissioners believe, invariably, been held in the capitals of the respective countries. In the present case it was peculiarly important that an undertaking which required the constant superintendence of a body of Commissioners, whose occupations for the most part confine them to London, should be carried on within their immediate cognisance, and not removed to a distant situation.

3. It being thus distinctly evident that the Exhibition ought to take place in London, it is further obvious that the actual site which may be selected for it should be within the precincts of, or in the closest vicinity to, the most central and accessible parts of the Metropolis itself. It need hardly be pointed out that it would be objectionable to impose upon persons who may have come to London from a great distance the necessity of an additional journey to visit the Exhibition; a consideration which has already been urged upon the Commissioners by the

representatives of several of the most important provincial towns, who are apprehensive of the inconvenience to which artizans in particular might thus be subjected. Moreover, the removal of the Exhibition to any distance sufficient to diminish the number of visitors would not only militate against its essential character of general accessibility, but might most seriously affect the receipts upon which its self-supporting character must depend, a point upon which it appears that much stress has been laid.

4. Although Hyde Park, and even the particular space now in question, had been already mentioned before the issue of the Commission, and indeed so far back as October, 1849, as a probable site for the Exhibition, it is unnecessary to assure the Lords of the Treasury that the Commissioners approached the question of the site after their appointment without having in any degree prejudged the merits of particular localities. On the 14th of February, their attention having been directed to the importance of determining the site by the Committee then recently appointed for all matters relating to the building, they deputed two Commissioners, namely, Lord Granville and Mr. Labouchere, to wait upon the Chief Commissioner of Woods and Forests, and to confer with him upon the subject. The result of this conference is set forth in the Report presented by the Building Committee at the next meeting of the Commissioners (Feb. 21), of which the following is the portion which relates to the question of the site:—

"With respect to the site, it has appeared to your Committee that, firstly, the north-eastern portion of Hyde Park; secondly, the long space between her Majesty's private road and the Kensington-road, in the southern part of Hyde Park; and, thirdly, the north-western portion of Regent's Park, are the only available spaces about the Metropolis which would afford the necessary accommodation; and it is believed that the order in which they have been named represents also their relative eligibility. As regards the first, the Committee are informed by the Chief Commissioner of her Majesty's Woods and Forests, that considerable objections would arise to its occupation for such a purpose, and that no such objections would be raised to the use of the second; the Committee, therefore, recommend the adoption of this site, which, amongst other advantages, is remarkable for the facility of access afforded by the existing roads. Upon this occasion a letter was received from the Westminster Committee, stating that the local Commissioners for Westminster had visited the site in Hyde Park, and a site suggested in the Regent's Park, and that they were of opinion that the site in Hyde Park was the preferable one."

The recommendation of the Building Committee having been agreed to, a form of advertisement, requesting plans and suggestions for the building, was, at the next meeting (28th February), submitted for approbation, and was ordered to be immediately issued in the English, French, and, German languages. To this advertisement was appended a ground-plan of the site in Hyde Park for the guidance of those to whom the advertisement was addressed. The details of this plan were discussed in the presence of the Chief Commissioner of Woods and Forests, and were settled in conformity with his lordship's wishes.

5. In consequence of the advertisement thus issued, no less than 248 plans and suggestions, many of them the productions of foreign artists, were sent in to the

Commissioners. A large number of these were of a very elaborate character, and bore evident marks of considerable application and ability.

6. Soon after the site had been selected, some other important arrangements having also by this time been made, the Commissioners prepared and published a statement (21 February) explanatory of the nature and objects of the Exhibition, which was widely circulated in this country, was forwarded to our consuls abroad and to the foreign consuls in England, and was officially transmitted by the Secretary of State to all Foreign Governments, and to all the Governors of the British Colonies, as well as to India. In this statement it was announced that "Her Majesty had been graciously pleased to grant a site for the purpose (of the Exhibition) on the south side of Hyde Park, lying between the Kensington Drive and the ride commonly called Rotten Row."

7. The site having been thus deliberately chosen and formally announced, all subsequent proceedings connected with the building have been taken with direct reference to it. The plans have been prepared with a view to its peculiarities, and the form of the building and its internal as well as its external arrangements have been determined by them. The amount of space available for the display of articles has been calculated upon the data afforded by the site, and from a calculation of this amount the Commissioners have been able to assign to each foreign country a definite space for the arrangement of its own productions. All the necessary working-drawings and specifications have been prepared with very great labour and at considerable expense, and have now been issued in a form which will insure to the Commissioners the certainty of obtaining, within a few days, *bonâ fide* tenders for the execution of a design presenting every facility for construction within the time prescribed. The mechanical difficulties have been surmounted, and all the preliminary arrangements, even to the extent of provision for an effective drainage and a sufficient water supply, have been entered into. The whole of these preparations have reference to this particular site only, and are inapplicable or unsuitable to any other.

8. From what has been already stated, it will be seen that the present site was not selected without consideration, and that the proceedings which have been taken with respect to it were not commenced until the Commissioners had good ground for believing that there would be no objection to its occupation. The attention, however, which has lately been directed to the point, has caused them anxiously to reconsider the whole subject, and renders it now necessary for them to enter into somewhat more of detail as to the grounds upon which they have come to the conclusion which they have formed, that this is the only site in or about the Metropolis which is at once suitable and practically available for the purposes of the Exhibition.

9. Of the other sites which have been suggested, the following are the only ones deserving of particular consideration:—

    (*a*) The North-eastern portion of Hyde Park.
    (*b*) The North-western portion of Regent's Park.
    (*c*) Battersea Park.

(*d*) Victoria Park.

(*e*) Wormwood Scrubbs.

10. The north-eastern portion of Hyde Park would, in the opinion of many members of the Building Committee, be a very eligible situation; but, as has been already mentioned, an objection was taken to this locality on the part of the Commissioners of Woods and Forests, on the ground that the building would interfere with some important thoroughfares in that part of the park, and on account of other considerations of public importance; and the idea was abandoned in consequence.

11. The site suggested in the Regent's Park has been found, since it was visited by the Building Committee, not to be available, as the leases under which the houses in the neighbourhood are held contain a clear and stringent provision that no new building of any kind shall be erected within the limits of the park.

12. With regard to the ground in the neighbourhood of Battersea proposed to be purchased by the Government, and to be converted into a park to be called Battersea Park, the Lords of the Treasury are of course aware that only a small proportion of the whole area has as yet been purchased; and the Commissioners found on inquiry that this proportion consists of numerous small detached pieces, utterly insufficient to accommodate a building of the contemplated size, and separated from each other by intervening plots of ground, many of them in a state of high cultivation, and belonging to a great number of different proprietors, with whom it would be absolutely impossible to effect arrangements within any time which would afford the slightest chance of the Commissioners being put in possession of a site in time to complete their building by the spring of next year. It should be added that the site of this district is very low, a great portion of it being some feet under high-water mark, and that the nature of the soil presents serious objections to its use as a building-ground.

13. Victoria Park is situated in an inconvenient and not very accessible part of the town. It would, moreover, be impossible to erect in it a building of the required size without most seriously interfering with the plantations and ornamental water which have been recently laid out there; thus inflicting on the classes for whose recreation that park has been opened an inconvenience infinitely more serious than could be caused to the frequenters of the very much larger area of Hyde Park by the proposed occupation of a comparatively small portion of it.

14. Lastly, as regards Wormwood Scrubbs, besides that the distance is a very serious objection, the rights of the commoners in that locality would prevent its appropriation; and the Commissioners are advised that it would be impossible to erect the building there without risk, as any single commoner would have it in his power to interrupt the proceedings, and to cause them to be discontinued at any stage of the work, however advanced. Similar objections apply to Wandsworth and some other commons in the neighbourhood of London, which have been occasionally mentioned as possible sites.

14*a*. As regards Primrose Hill and the Isle of Dogs, the want of level space on the former, and the objectionable situation and dampness of the latter, render them so obviously unsuitable as to make any particular observations unnecessary.

15. But even could the objections to any of these sites be removed, or could another and an unobjectionable site be pointed out, the Commissioners feel hound to state, from their experience of the time, thought, and labour necessarily consumed in the investigation, arrangement, and preparation of the great mass of detail requisite to enable them to carry out this extensive work, that they are fully convinced of the impossibility of now adapting their plans to any other site, with any reasonable prospect of being able to complete the work within the time to which they stand pledged in the face of the world; and they could only regard a change of site, particularly if it should involve a change of plan, as tantamount to the postponement of the Exhibition till another year. And the Commissioners cannot shut their eyes to the fact, that a postponement of the Exhibition would, under the circumstances, certainly lead to its entire abandonment.

16. In order to give the Lords of the Treasury some idea of the consequences of an abandonment of this scheme, the Commissioners would in the first place direct their attention to the large amount of money already subscribed towards its completion (which is at present nearly 64,000*l.*), to the number of local committees (now about 240) which have been called into existence throughout the country, to the funds now being raised by subscriptions out of their wages among the working-classes in all parts of the country towards enabling them to visit an Exhibition to which they are anxiously looking forward, and the abandonment of which would be a great disappointment to numbers, and still more to the extensive preparations which are now making for the supply of articles for exhibition. It is within the knowledge of the Commissioners that several individuals in this country have incurred several thousand pounds' expense in such preparations, besides the anxiety which they have occasioned.

17. But the evils which would result from postponement, so far as this country is concerned, are as nothing when compared with those which would arise in the case of foreign nations and the colonies. The plan of the Exhibition has been widely circulated for several months, and the following States have already signified, through their respective Governments, that they have appointed Committees or Commissioners, consisting of the most distinguished individuals in those countries, to co-operate with the Royal Commissioners in this country:—

Russia,	Hanover,	The United States,
Sweden,	Oldenburg,	Turkey,
Norway,	Mecklenburg,	Sardinia,
Denmark,	Hanse Towns,	Venezuela,
Prussia,	France,	Switzerland,
Saxony,	Holland,	Nassau,
Austria,	Belgium,	Anhalt, Dessau, &c.
Bavaria,	Spain,	

Besides which it may be mentioned that special Commissioners have been sent to this country by France, Russia, and one or two other States; and that in most cases the Governments have undertaken the collection and the transmission to this country, at their own expense, of the articles intended for exhibition, for which, of course, their preparations are now made.

18. In all the countries which have been mentioned active preparations for the Exhibition are now going on, and in some considerable expense is known to have been incurred. The Russian Government has announced that the goods intended for exhibition will be shipped from that country in the autumn of this year, and questions pointing to a similar arrangement have recently been put by the Government of Denmark. The Austrian Government have given notice, that the Great Exhibition which was to have been held at Vienna in the year 1851 has been postponed till the year 1852, in order not to clash with the Exhibition in London. All these circumstances tend to show that the postponement of the Exhibition would be seriously inconvenient to many countries, and would probably occasion considerable and natural irritation at what would appear like national vacillation, besides the certainty of rendering these countries unwilling to run the risk of a second disappointment, and of deterring them from continuing their preparations for a later period.

19. These inconveniences would be felt also by the British Colonies. Committees have been announced as formed in Malta, Ceylon, Nova Scotia, Barbadoes, Guiana, and several of the West India Islands, and it is probable that others have been appointed elsewhere. In India most extensive preparations are being made, and the East India Company have incurred very great expense by their exertions to contribute to the Exhibition.

20. After what has been said, it is unnecessary that the Commissioners should enlarge any further upon the consequences to be apprehended from the postponement which would be occasioned by an alteration of the site of building. They will proceed to offer a few remarks upon some of the objections which have been taken to that at present proposed.

21. An idea appears to prevail in some quarters that the occupation of the Park is intended to be of a permanent, and not, as has been repeatedly announced, of a merely temporary character, and the Commissioners are given to understand that by proposing to construct a building into which a good deal of brickwork is to enter, they have shown an intention at variance with their professions. Upon this point they have to remark, in the first place, that, although the eminent architects and engineers whom they have consulted, and to whom they have uniformly given instructions to prepare plans suitable to a temporary structure, have agreed to recommend the use of brick and other durable materials, they have left it perfectly open to contractors to send in their tenders for the execution of the work in any material or materials whatsoever, and have notified their readiness to entertain such tenders, on the single condition of their being "accompanied by working-drawings and specifications, and fully priced bills of quantities." It is probable that some such tenders will be made, and if made they will be impartially considered; but the Commissioners must protest against the supposition that it is necessarily more judicious to construct a temporary building of perishable than of enduring materials. The first requisite of the building is, that it should be suitable for its purpose, capable of protecting the valuable goods deposited in it from inju-

ry of every kind — as, for instance, from the weather, from the effects of the dampness of the soil, from the danger of fire, and so forth, and that it should be strong enough to avert all risk of accidental damage. Its next requisite is, that it should be economical, and in estimating its cost regard must be had not only to the expense of erection, but to the facility of removal and the value of the materials when removed, as a building may easily be conceived to be cheaper which should cost 100,000*l.* to erect, but of which the materials could afterwards be sold for 50,000*l.*, than another would be which cost but 80,000*l.* in the first instance, but of which the materials should become so far deteriorated as to produce only 20,000*l.* when taken down. It is the opinion of those who have devised the plans in the present case, that a building constructed of durable materials will in the end be cheaper than one constructed of such as are more perishable; particularly as a considerable portion of the building, namely, the iron roofing, will be of a kind which is generally used in the construction of railway-stations, and will probably be disposed of for that purpose after the close of the Exhibition, as its temporary application to the purposes of the Exhibition will be of no detriment to its being so. An opportunity of testing the correctness of this opinion will be given when the tenders are received, as, in addition to the customary form, it has been required that they should also be sent upon the understanding that the materials shall remain the property of the contractor, and shall in fact only be hired for the purposes of the Exhibition. The third requisite of the building is, that it should be at least seemly, though it may not be necessary that it should be highly ornamental. The Commissioners trust that it will fulfil this condition, while they would at the same time point out that no expense is to be incurred for merely ornamental purposes, unless it should be thought desirable to select a dome for covering in the large space which must necessarily be left in the centre of the building to suit the internal arrangements. A cheaper mode of covering in this space will probably be resorted to, and the Commissioners have directed that a special estimate of the cost of the dome should be laid before them when the tenders are complete, in order that they may judge of the propriety of sanctioning its erection.

Having offered this short explanation, they can only repeat once more the assurances they have already given, that the building is not intended to be permanent, and that it will be entirely removed, in accordance with the conditions prescribed by the Lords of the Treasury on yielding up the site, within seven months after the closing of the Exhibition, which cannot be deferred after the 1st of November, and will probably take place at an earlier period in the autumn of next year.

22. Another ground of apprehension is stated to be, lest the Park should be injured by the erection of the building, and the injury should continue after the structure is removed. This apprehension is, however, groundless; a small clump of ten trees has been allowed to be removed, in compensation for which, it is proposed by the Commissioners of Woods and Forests to plant another clump elsewhere. It is not intended to cut down any more than that clump. As regards the surface of the ground to be occupied, it will not only not be injured, but will ultimately be materially improved by being drained and freshly sown with grass

seed. It will be a strict condition with the contractors for the building that they shall, on its removal, restore the ground to its present condition.

23. Some dissatisfaction has been expressed at the prospect of a furnace being erected to heat the boiler and drive the steam-apparatus. It is however, intended to construct such furnace on the principle of consuming its own smoke, or to burn coke instead of coal, should that, upon the whole, appear the best mode of preventing annoyance. Care will also be taken not to erect any chimney of an unsightly character.

24. As regards the amount of traffic which will be occasioned by the transport of materials and goods to the site, the Commissioners have been furnished by the Building Committee with an approximate estimate that it will not in the whole exceed the ordinary amount of three weeks' general traffic of a single railway-station, and as this traffic will be spread over a period of more than six months, it is manifest that its amount has been enormously exaggerated by public estimation.

25. The Queen's Ride, though in the immediate vicinity of the site, will not be in any degree interfered with, except that it may be advisable to rail off a strip not exceeding ten feet, or one-sixth of the whole in width, for foot-passengers, in order to prevent the inconvenience of crowding the space open to riding parties. By this arrangement the riders will be secured from annoyance.

25 *a.* It has been said that the effect of the erection of the building will be to drive the inhabitants of London out of their Parks. The Commissioners think it right to draw the attention of the Lords of the Treasury to the following statistics:—

The area of Hyde Park is	387	acres.
The area of Kensington Gardens	290	acres.
The area of Regent's Park	403	acres.
The area of St. James's Park	83	acres.
The area of Green Park	71	acres.
The area of Victoria Park	160	acres.
The area of Greenwich Park	174	acres.

making a total of 1,568 acres, while only twenty acres are proposed to be taken or the purposes of this Exhibition.

26. In conclusion, the Commissioners think it desirable to call attention to the fact, that the three last Exhibitions of this nature which have taken place in Paris have been held on a site (the Champs Elysées) very closely corresponding to our own Hyde Park in many respects, and particularly resembling it in being the most fashionable and the most frequented promenade in Paris—more frequented, indeed, than the particular spot selected on the present occasion has ever been, or is likely to be; and yet it does not appear that the Parisians have had occasion to complain of those annoyances which are now apprehended by some persons in this country. And the Commissioners are informed, that the Exhibition in Vienna was held in the Prado, the principal public place in that city; and that the Exhibition in Berlin was held in the Thiergarten, which is not only the principal public

place within the city, but is remarkable as being the only open Park of any sort within several miles.

27. In the foregoing observations the Commissioners have thought it right to confine themselves strictly to a discussion of the practical difficulties which would attend a change of site. They cannot, however, but express their decided opinion, that the renouncement of the selection of the most beautiful park in London for the scene of the Exhibition may be looked upon as indicating a diminution of interest in the undertaking, and would materially detract from that appearance of hospitality on the part of England which has been one great cause for the very favourable reception which this proposal has everywhere secured.

They must add, that the possibility that the bringing the Exhibition into Hyde Park should be considered as an interference with the enjoyment of that Park by the public has never entered their minds. They have, on the contrary, always intended it as a means of recreative and intellectual enjoyment for the greatest portion of her Majesty's subjects: and they have hitherto had reason to believe that it has been so regarded by the country in general.

REPORT OF THE ROYAL COMMISSIONERS, PRESENTED TO HER MAJESTY ON THE OPENING OF THE BUILDING.

The following Report, together with her Majesty's Answer, on the occasion of the inauguration of the building, cannot fail to be interesting as a brief record of the proceedings connected with this noble undertaking up to that period:—

"May it please your Majesty,—We, the Commissioners appointed by your Majesty's royal warrant of the 3rd of January, 1850, for the promotion of the Exhibition of the Works of Industry of all Nations, and subsequently incorporated by your Majesty's Royal Charter of the 15th of August in the same year, humbly beg leave, on the occasion of your Majesty's auspicious visit at the opening of the Exhibition, to lay before you a brief statement of our proceedings to the present time.

"By virtue of the authority graciously committed to us by your Majesty, we have made diligent inquiry into the matters which your Majesty was pleased to refer to us, namely, into the best mode of introducing the productions of your Majesty's colonies and of foreign countries into this kingdom, the selection of the most suitable site for the Exhibition, the general conduct of the undertaking, and the proper method of determining the nature of the prizes and of securing the most impartial distribution of them.

"In the prosecution of these inquiries, and in the discharge of the duties assigned to us by your Majesty's Royal Charter of Incorporation, we have held constant meetings of our whole body, and have, moreover, referred numerous questions connected with a great variety of subjects to committees, composed partly of our own members and partly of individuals distinguished in the several departments of science and the arts, who have cordially responded to our applications for their assistance at a great sacrifice of their valuable time.

"Among the earliest questions brought before us was the important one as to the terms upon which articles offered for exhibition should be admitted into the building. We considered that it was a main characteristic of the national undertaking in which we were engaged that it should depend wholly upon the voluntary contributions of the people of this country for its success; and we therefore decided, without hesitation, that no charge whatever should be made on the admission of such goods. We considered, also, that the office of selecting the articles to be sent should be intrusted in the first instance to local committees, to be established in every foreign country, and in various districts of your Majesty's dominions; a general power of control being reserved to the Commission.

"We have now the gratification of stating that our anticipations of support in this course have in all respects been fully realised. Your Majesty's most gracious donation to the funds of the Exhibition was the signal for voluntary contributions from all, even the humblest, classes of your subjects, and the funds which have thus been placed at our disposal amount at present to about 65,000*l*. Local committees, from which we have uniformly received the most zealous co-operation, were formed in all parts of the United Kingdom, in many of your Majesty's colonies, and in the territories of the Hon. East India Company. The most energetic support has also been received from the Governments of nearly all the countries of the world, in most of which Commissions have been appointed for the special purpose of promoting the objects of an Exhibition justly characterised in your Majesty's royal warrant as an Exhibition of the Works of Industry of all Nations.

"We have also to acknowledge the great readiness with which persons of all classes have come forward as exhibitors. And here again it becomes our duty to return our humble thanks to your Majesty for the most gracious manner in which your Majesty has condescended to associate yourself with your subjects by yourself contributing some most valuable and interesting articles to the Exhibition.

"The number of exhibitors whose productions it has been found possible to accommodate is about 15,000, of whom nearly one-half are British. The remainder represent the productions of more than forty foreign countries, comprising almost the whole of the civilised nations of the globe. In arranging the space to be allotted to each, we have taken into consideration both the nature of its productions and the facilities of access to this country afforded by its geographical position. Your Majesty will find the productions of your Majesty's dominions arranged in the western portion of the building, and those of foreign countries in the eastern. The Exhibition is divided into the four great classes of—1, Raw Materials; 2, Machinery; 3, Manufactures; and 4, Sculpture and the Fine Arts. A further division has been made according to the geographical position of the countries represented; those which lie within the warmer latitudes being placed near the centre of the building, and the colder countries at the extremities.

"Your Majesty having been graciously pleased to grant a site in this your royal Park for the purposes of the Exhibition, the first column of the structure now honoured by your Majesty's presence was fixed on the 26th of September last. Within the short period, therefore, of seven months, owing to the energy of the contractors and the active industry of the workmen employed by them, a building has been erected, entirely novel in its construction, covering a space of more than eighteen acres, measuring 1,851 feet in length, and 456 feet in extreme breadth, capable of containing 40,000 visitors, and affording a frontage for the exhibition of goods to the extent of more than ten miles. For the original suggestion of the principle of this structure the Commissioners are indebted to Mr. Joseph Paxton, to whom they feel their acknowledgments to be justly due for this interesting feature of their undertaking.

"With regard to the distribution of rewards to deserving exhibitors, we have decided that they should be given in the form of medals, not with reference to merely individual competition, but as rewards for excellence in whatever shape it may present itself. The selection of the persons to be so rewarded has been intrusted to juries equally composed of British subjects and of foreigners, the former having been selected by the Commission from the recommendations made by the local committees, and the latter by the Governments of the foreign nations the productions of which are exhibited. The names of these jurors, comprising, as they do, many of European celebrity, afford the best guarantee of the impartiality with which the rewards will be assigned.

"It affords much gratification that, notwithstanding the magnitude of this undertaking, and the great distances from which many of the articles now exhibited have had to be collected, the day on which your Majesty has been graciously pleased to be present at the inauguration of the Exhibition is the same day that was originally named for its opening, thus affording a proof of what may, under God's blessing, be accomplished by goodwill and cordial co-operation among nations, aided by the means that modern science has placed at our command.

"Having thus briefly laid before your Majesty the results of our labours, it now only remains for us to convey to your Majesty our dutiful and loyal acknowledgments of the support and encouragement which we have derived throughout this extensive and laborious task from the gracious favour and countenance of your Majesty. It is our heartfelt prayer that this undertaking, which has for its end the promotion of all branches of human industry and the strengthening of the bonds of peace and friendship among all nations of the earth, may, by the blessing of Divine Providence, conduce to the welfare of your Majesty's people, and be long remembered among the brightest circumstances of your Majesty's peaceful and happy reign."

Her Majesty returned the following gracious answer:—

"I receive with the greatest satisfaction the address which you have presented to me on the opening of this Exhibition.

"I have observed with a warm and increasing interest the progress of your proceedings in the execution of the duties intrusted to you by the Royal Commission, and it affords me sincere gratification to witness the successful result of your judicious and unremitting exertions in the splendid spectacle by which I am this day surrounded.

"I cordially concur with you in the prayer, that by God's blessing this undertaking may conduce to the welfare of my people and to the common interest of the human race, by encouraging the arts of peace and industry, strengthening the bonds of union among the nations of the earth, and promoting a friendly and honourable rivalry in the useful exercise of those faculties which have been conferred by a beneficent Providence for the good and the happiness of mankind."

THE END.

Lector House believes that a society develops through a two-fold approach of continuous learning and adaptation, which is derived from the study of classic literary works spread across the historic timeline of literature records. Therefore, we aim at reviving, repairing and redeveloping all those inaccessible or damaged but historically as well as culturally important literature across subjects so that the future generations may have an opportunity to study and learn from past works to embark upon a journey of creating a better future.

This book is a result of an effort made by Lector House towards making a contribution to the preservation and repair of original ancient works which might hold historical significance to the approach of continuous learning across subjects.

HAPPY READING & LEARNING!

LECTOR HOUSE LLP
E-MAIL: lectorpublishing@gmail.com